D1483690

HISTORY AND HERALDRY
1254 TO 1310

HISTORY AND HERALDRY

1254 to 1310

A STUDY OF THE HISTORICAL VALUE
OF THE ROLLS OF ARMS

BY

N. DENHOLM-YOUNG

OXFORD
AT THE CLARENDON PRESS
1965

Oxford University Press, Amen House, London E.C.4

GLASGOW NEW YORK TORONTO MELBOURNE WELLINGTON
BOMBAY CALCUTTA MADRAS KARACHI LAHORE DACCA
CAPE TOWN SALISBURY NAIROBI IBADAN ACCRA
KUALA LUMPUR HONG KONG

ACKNOWLEDGEMENTS

My best thanks are due to Sir Anthony Wagner, Garter Principal King of Arms, for many kindnesses. It will be obvious to all who use Sir Anthony's *Catalogue of English Medieval Rolls of Arms*, cited as *CEMRA*, how deeply I am indebted to its thorough and exact scholarship. I also owe much to Mr. T. D. Tremlett, Secretary of the Society of Antiquaries, for allowing me to impound over a long period his copies of St. George's Roll and Collins' Roll (Duke of Gloucester's version) from College of Arms MS. 14. Mr. W. J. Smith very kindly allowed me to use his thesis, which I have inadvertently omitted to cite, on the armies of King John, and Mr. Brindley Parry, Archivist of Caernarvon, has assisted me almost daily in this as in other publications.

N. D.-Y.

14 January 1965

CONTENTS

VI. SIR ROBERT CLIFFORD AND THE ROLLS
(i) Clifford and Collins' Roll ... 96
(ii) Falkirk Roll ... 103

VII. CLIFFORD AGAIN
(i) Clifford from 1298 to 1308 ... 112
(ii) Nativity Roll ... 116
(iii) Labels ... 118

VIII. THE CONSTABLE, THE MARSHAL, AND THE *CURIA MILITARIS* ... 120

IX. THE DUNSTABLE TOURNAMENT ROLL ... 125

X. KNIGHTS OF THE SHIRE AND SHERIFFS ... 147
(i) Knights of the Shire ... 150
(ii) Sheriffs ... 152

LIST OF WORKS CITED ... 160

APPENDIX ... 166

INDEX ... 167

ABBREVIATIONS

Anct. Corr.	List of Ancient Correspondence (PRO, Lists and Indexes, no. XV), 1902.
Ann. Burton	Annales monasterii de Burton in *Annales monastici*, I (RS).
Ann. Lond.	Annales Londonienses in *Chronicles of the Reigns of Edward I and II* (RS).
Ann. Paul.	Annales Paulini, ibid.
Ann. Theok.	Annales monasterii de Theokesburia in *Ann. mon.* I.
Ann. Wigorn.	Annales monasterii de Wigornia in *Ann. mon.* II.
Ann. Wint.	Annales monasterii de Wintonia in *Ann. mon.* II.
Arch.	Archaeological, *Archaeologia*.
Arg.	Argent.
Az.	Azure.
Bar.	*Baronage.*
Barth. Cott.	*Bartholomei de Cotton Historia Anglicana*, ed. Luard (RS), 1859.
BIHR	*Bulletin of the Institute of Historical Research.*
Cal. Cl. R.	*Calendar of Close Rolls.*
Cal. Docs. Scot.	J. Bain, *Calendar of Documents relating to Scotland.*
Cal. IPM	*Calendar of Inquisitiones post mortem* (PRO).
Cal. Pap. Lett.	W. H. Bliss, *Calendar of Entries in the Papal Registers relating to Great Britain and Ireland*, I, 1893.
CDS	See J. Bain, *Cal. Docs. Scot.*
CEMRA	*A Catalogue of English Medieval Rolls of Arms*, by A. Wagner (Society of Antiquaries), 1950; published as vol. i of *Aspilogia: being Materials of Heraldry.*
CFR	*Calendar of Fine Rolls, 1272–1337*, 4 vols., 1911–13.
Chron. Ed. I & II	*Chronicles of the Reigns of Edward I and II* (RS).

Chron. Maj. v, *Addit.*	Matthew Paris, *Chronica Majora,* v, Additamenta.
Chron. T. Wykes	Chronicon vulgo dictum Chronicon Thomæ Wykes in *Ann. mon.* III (RS).
Cl. R.	*Close Rolls.*
Coll. Top. et Gen.	*Collectanea Topographica et Genealogica.*
Cott. MS.	Cottonian Manuscript, British Museum.
CPR	*Calendar of Patent Rolls* (PRO).
D.B., i	W. Dugdale, *The Baronage of England,* i.
DNB	*Dictionary of National Biography.*
EHR	*English Historical Review.*
Enc. Brit.	*Encyclopaedia Britannica.*
Erm.	Ermine.
Exc. e Rot. Fin.	*Excerpta e Rotulis Finium, 1216–1272,* ed. Charles Roberts, 2 vols. (Record Commission), 1835–6.
Flores	*Flores Historiarum,* ed. Luard, 3 vols. (RS), 1890.
Fl. Wig. Cont.	*Florentii Wigorniensis Monachi Chronicon ex Chronicis,* ed. B. Thorpe, 2 vols., 1848.
Foed.	T. Rymer, *Foedera, Conventions etc.,* I–III (Record Commission), 1816–19.
G.E.C.	G. E. Cokayne, *The Complete Peerage,* new ed. by Vicary Gibbs & others, 1910–59.
Gerv. Cant.	*The Historical Works of Gervase of Canterbury* (RS).
Hants Rec. Soc.	Hampshire Record Society.
Hem.	Hemingburgh.
Hist. MSS. Comm. Rep.	Historical Manuscripts Commission Reports.
IPM	*Inquisitio post mortem.*
Lib. de Ant. Leg.	*De Antiquis Legibus Liber: Chronica maiorum et vicecomitum Londoniarum,* ed. T. Stapleton (Camden Society), 1846.
Linc. Rec. Soc.	Lincoln Record Society.
Matt. Par., *Chron. Maj.*	*Matthaei Parisiensis Chronica Majora,* ed. Luard, 7 vols. (RS), 1872–83.
Matt. Par., *Hist. Anglorum*	*Historia Anglorum,* ed. Sir F. Madden, 3 vols. (RS), 1866–9.
OED	*Oxford English Dictionary.*

NS	New Series.
Parl. Writs	F. Palgrave, *Parliamentary Writs and Writs of Military Summons, Edward I and Edward II* (Record Commission), 1827–34.
PQW	*Placita de Quo Warranto* (Record Commission), 1818.
PRA	Parliamentary Roll of Arms.
PRO	Public Record Office.
PS	Privy Seal.
QRMR, KRMR	Queen's or King's Remembrancer's Memoranda Roll (PRO).
R. lit. cl.	*Rotuli litterarum clausarum, 1204–27*, ed. T. D. Hardy, 2 vols. (Record Commission), 1833 and 1834.
R. lit. pat.	*Rotuli litterarum patentium, 1201–16*, ed. T. D. Hardy (Record Commission), 1838.
Rot. chart.	*Rotuli Chartarum, 1199–1216* (Record Commission), 1837.
Rot. Hund.	*Rotuli Hundredorum tempore Henrici III et Edwardi I*, 2 vols. (Record Commission), 1812–18.
Rot. Norm.	*Rotuli Normanniae, 1200–5* (Record Commission), 1835.
RS	Rolls Series.
Sa.	Sable.
Song	*The Roll of Caerlaverock*, ed. T. Wright, 1864.
T.R. Hist. Soc.	*Transactions of the Royal Historical Society.*
VCH	*Victoria County History of England.*
Wav.	Annales of Waverley, ed. Luard, in *Ann. mon.* ii.
Wendover	*Roger de Wendover, Flores Historiarum, to 1235*, ed. H.O. Coxe (English Historical Society), 1841-4.

I

PROVENANCE AND HISTORICAL VALUE OF THE ROLLS

HEREIN is attempted a reintegration of heraldry and history in the light of the surviving Rolls of Arms made in the lifetime of Edward I and the early years of Edward II, between about 1252 and 1309. Only five of these rolls exist in contemporary manuscripts. These are the mutilated remains of the Heralds' Roll, Camden's Roll, the Dering Roll, the *Song of Caerlaverock*, and the Parliamentary Roll of Arms. The authenticity of others is vouched for by copies made in the sixteenth and seventeenth centuries by Robert Glover and Sir William Dugdale. A few raise textual problems that are discussed as they arise, and considered in much greater detail in the *Catalogue of English Medieval Rolls of Arms*.

The number of chivalrous persons whom these Rolls were intended to commemorate was in my view not greatly increased by the great economic and social progress made since the Conquest. How complete the evidence is we cannot say, but it would be difficult to recover the names of more than 2,000 knights in any one year, and of these not all were 'strenuous'. There was a shortage of such persons throughout the period, and the whole class of lay gentry, i.e. those with an income thought by the king and his advisers to be sufficient to bear the burden of knighthood, contained, it is thought, hardly more than three times this number, or roughly the equivalent of the known number of knight's fees in the country. The great increase of population was in the towns. It is probable that in this period the use of armorial bearings was confined to the 'strenuous' knights, i.e. those who had seen or hoped to see military action, including warlike prelates like Anthony Bek. The armigerous class is a small one, for men did not 'assume arms' for decorative or social reasons. The armour was for defence, and the heraldic coat an aid to recognition in the field. We are dealing with a small body of professional soldiers, known to their contemporaries as 'strenuous knights'.[1]

The names of such men, and their coats of arms, are preserved in Rolls of Arms. These are sometimes in book form, but to all the generic term 'Rolls of Arms' is applied. It will be seen that the period covered by the Rolls concerned extends some three years after the death of Edward I in 1307, for the work of his heralds was not completed until it found expression in the orderly and comprehensive Roll known to modern scholars as the Parliamentary Roll of Arms. This is the period when heraldry came most closely into the life of the king and his knights: when these lists of earls, barons, and knights were made, usually in no sort of order, with their armorial bearings on painted shields or banners, or in blazon (that is, described in the technical language of the heralds). Later copies are often 'in trick', whereby the arms are sketched and the colours indicated by conventional symbols.

Few original rolls, in the exact sense of the word, except the Boroughbridge Roll of 1322, were produced after the PRA. The next generation preferred to produce classified lists, arranged according to the nature of the charge upon the shield. These Ordinaries, as they are called, begin with Cooke's Ordinary of c. 1340.

The PRA itself is our greatest and most authoritative Roll, 'bearing as it does all the marks of an official survey'.[2]

---

[1] An early instance is found under 1236 in *The Red Book of the Exchequer* (R.S.), ii. 756, when Nicholas de Molis and Richard Siward as *milites strenui* bore the two sceptres at the coronation of the Queen. Was the phrase *miles literatus*, common in Matthew Paris, perhaps used by way of contrast?

[2] *CEMRA*, p. xvi.

It is neatly arranged by counties. But even this document (it is in book form in the earliest extant version) has a deficiency in common with the bulk of medieval records in that there is no trace of alphabetical order. It is difficult to imagine why it never occurred to anyone at any time to put these lists of princes, earls, barons, and knights into alphabetical order. Perhaps authors were discouraged by the astonishing number of ways in which even a simple name could be spelt. At any rate, apart from the PRA the only signs of logical arrangement are in the Falkirk Roll, drawn up by 'battles' or brigades, and the Dunstable Roll, which names the earls and their retinues as they occur.

These rolls, varying in length from less than a hundred to more than a thousand names, were works of art produced at leisure by professional heralds either for their own use or for patrons interested in chivalrous achievements; but they are here used to serve a much wider purpose. For this book is an attempt to integrate the Rolls of Arms with the social and political history of the age in which they were produced. This is a simple task when the so-called Occasional Rolls, or rolls of tournaments, sieges, or battles are in question; but there are a number of general rolls, whose provenance is obscure (though the search for it is fascinating). None of them is an official document; we do not know that the heralds were ever asked to complete a list of the knights of Edward I. Rolls of arms, particularly perhaps painted rolls, were probably at all times a luxury, certainly not part of the essential machinery of government, as were Marshalsea rolls or Chancery rolls. The purpose of our rolls was purely heraldic, and they were always private property to be bought and sold and devised by will. The rolls could be colourful, romantic, and possibly snobbish, and until we come to the end of our story their lack of arrangement precludes the idea that they were compiled for use in the field.

This form of heraldic art leaps into prominence in the mid-thirteenth century, at about the time when bannerets are first heard of in military history. They were compiled, I suppose (as Dugdale would say), by royal or seignorial heralds in their private capacity, and their first object must have been to gratify the patron who employed them. They may be regarded as the by-products of heraldic expertise, which was professionally engaged in proclaiming, marshalling, or prohibiting tournaments, and in assisting at weddings, funerals, and coronations.

It appears that the distinction between the heralds and the minstrels was still hard to draw. The diplomatic functions of the heralds as envoys, sometimes accompanying ambassadors, are not attested in the records that have been examined for our period.

It may come as a surprise to some that these Rolls of Arms are so often based upon no discoverable principle and enlarged from time to time by agglomeration. It is common enough in many classes of medieval records. An annoying feature is that, though earls and counts are usually so styled, bachelors are rarely distinguished from bannerets. A banneret is only distinguishable when he displays his banner on the field of battle, or when it is painted in lieu of a shield upon a roll of arms.

It is not necessary to imagine that Henry III deliberately encouraged the growth of heraldry, any more than that Edward I encouraged tournaments. Heraldry, and everything that went with it, was part of the climate in which they lived, and shields of arms were a natural form of decoration for the king's palaces at Westminster, including the Abbey, or Winchester (1240–65), or the king's Great Chamber at the Tower. Armorial glass was ordered with the king's shield and that of the late Count of Provence for Rochester Castle in 1247, and for the palace at Havering atte Bower in 1251 and 1268.[1] These are contemporary with the literary and pictorial evidence scattered through the works of Matthew Paris, whose

---

[1] A. G. and W. O. Hassall, *The Douce Apocalypse* (1962), p. 8. The details are from the printed Liberate Rolls.

collection of painted shields (*c.* 1244) is the earliest extant English heraldic monument.

Evidence for shields of arms appears from about 1130, and increases rapidly during the 'Anarchy' of Stephen's reign, in close association with the as yet unorganized 'mass-tournament' of which the king was said to be inordinately fond. When a much stricter control of tournaments was imposed by Richard I in 1194, greater opportunities were provided for the emergence of professional heralds, who 'travelled through the country and even abroad to proclaim a forthcoming event, made the arrangements, announced the competitors, kept the score, declared the victors, and marshalled the processions to and from the lists'. These are the words of a recent writer,[1] himself a herald, but how much of it is applicable to the thirteenth century? It cannot have been royal heralds who proclaimed tournaments of which perhaps 75 per cent. were at once prohibited by the King's Messenger. Is there any evidence, other than the scraps indicated in this book, for the existence of baronial heralds who did all this in the thirteenth century in England? Tournaments come fully into view only in 1194 and 1215. In the latter year a lady presented the prize, a bear, and this is the first scrap of evidence seen for what might be termed a local tournament, as opposed to one that roamed all over the countryside. From that time, at least, there must have been persons to organize the proceedings, but the heralds are not spoken of until the rules for tournaments emerge in the *Statutum Armorum* of *c.* 1265, which is about a decade later than our first Roll of Arms.

These rolls[2] were rarely treated as sacrosanct by the heralds. They were made to be used, and they were copied in whole or in part, with or without additions and inter-

---

[1] Scott-Giles, *How to look at Heraldry* (1962), p. 5.

[2] The term 'Roll of Arms' is the generic term given to manuscript records of armorial bearings whether in roll or (as with the *Song of Caerlaverock* and the PRA) book form, and for convenience embraces the Matthew Paris shields scattered throughout that author's works.

polations at later dates. So there are few rolls that do not present a variety of textual problems. Every working herald had to keep his information up to date and possibly to glorify a person or family by the retrospective discovery of noble forebears and, always, of noble associations. In the thirteenth century this jactatory urge was satisfied by seemingly haphazard lists of earls and other persons long dead, and by the introduction of Arthurian heroes or other fabulous persons. A few very late rolls are spurious compilations or students' exercises. It was not until the later fifteenth century that rolls of arms were self-consciously falsified by interpolation for political or dynastic purposes.

For our period nothing is known of the position of heralds in England with regard to the assumption of arms by non-armigerous persons, or of the right to adjudicate between rival claimants to the same arms; or what authority, if any, Kings of Arms exercised over subordinate heralds or minstrels. These matters come to light only in a later period.

Many of the rolls and other heraldic collections have always been the property of heralds, handed down or bought and sold as their stock in trade, or working capital. Hence they have come to be known, since antiquaries started to write about them, and even before, by the names of their owners, or former owners and efforts to classify them have led to renaming them, often more than once. These names have become a source of confusion and a stumbling-block, and conceal the fact that divergent types of historical document are in question, and that some rolls are of great interest to the historian and others are not. The Parliamentary Roll, for example, is a manuscript book in the British Museum, and is so called because Palgrave printed it among the Parliamentary Writs. It is in no sense a list of persons summoned to Parliament, and except by way of comparison with lists of members has no bearing upon the history of parliamentary institutions.

It is a matter for surprise that none of these rolls—
except the PRA—appears to have emanated from the
royal court. It might have been expected that the tournament at Blyth where the Lord Edward figured as a novice
in 1256, before his first active service in Gwynedd in
August of that year, or the even greater tournament at
Nefyn in 1284, or even the 'little battle of Chalon' in
1273, would have been commemorated by the heralds. But
no heraldic activity is recorded in connexion with these
events, nor has any roll survived.

With few exceptions ecclesiastics do not appear. The
arms of William, bishop-elect of Valence, are given by
Metthew Paris.[1] Anthony Bek, Patriarch of Jerusalem
and Bishop of Durham, is on the Heralds' Roll and the
PRA. As a Palatine earl he probably had his own herald.
There are a scattering of Welsh, Scottish, and Irish
knights, and some rolls (especially the Heralds' Roll,
Camden's Roll, and the Dering Roll) include many
foreign coats, particularly from France and Flanders.

It will be clear that as historical documents the rolls
vary much in value, since some (Occasional rolls) include
only living persons, while others span two or more generations and include mythical persons to glorify the patron by
association. For it must be assumed that the heralds, like
the minstrel class out of which they had emerged, produced their beautifully painted rolls because they were
paid to gratify the tastes of their patrons. They needed
blazoned rolls as part of their stock in trade, but the
painted rolls must have been sponsored by someone. The
Occasional rolls of battles, sieges, or tournaments might
have had a ready sale, or could have been commissioned
by a successful protagonist. But the provenance of the
general rolls is usually a matter of great obscurity, though
in at least one case the search has proved rewarding. Did
a great man never ask for a roll of his friends, his com-
panions in arms, his tenants or his retainers? We shall

---

[1] Matthew Paris, *Hist. Anglorum*, iii. 427; *Chron. Maj. Addit.* vi. 477.

perhaps never know. But some of the general rolls can be associated more particularly with one march rather than another, made perhaps as much for the use of the herald himself in the pursuit of his professional duties, to prevent the duplication of coats, or the use of arms by unauthorized persons within the province or march for which he was responsible. To say this is to assume what is still incapable of proof, but fragmentary evidence is slowly coming to light.

The roll such as Collins' Roll, which can be dated by internal evidence as having been compiled about 1296, was possibly drawn up, or commissioned, while the compiler was serving as herald to Sir Robert Clifford. The herald celebrates his master by putting his name immediately after the list of earls, though he was only 18 or 19 at the time and the preceding battle of Dunbar is the first action in which he is known to have taken part. The opportunity for the compilation of such a roll was provided by that great assembly of English and Scottish notables at Berwick in 1296. The list thus made, commemorating Edward I's victory at Dunbar, the abdication of John Balliol from the throne of Scotland,[1] the arrival of a distinguished Irish contingent, and the capture of a rich haul of Scottish prisoners, would be of great value to a herald for future reference, though in no sense an Occasional roll. Such a chance might not come twice in the lifetime of a herald. Probably there would be a ready market for such a document, tailored, so to speak, to fit the customer, with another than Clifford taking pride of place as opportunity offered. It may be imagined that if it had been arranged by counties, as was by a touch of genius the PRA, it would have been chopped up into sections like that great roll and interpolated to meet local needs. A

[1] Balliol is not included in the roll. He lost his rank and lived the life of a country gentleman in the south of England, indulging in no more warlike pursuit than hunting in Surrey. He enjoyed most of the amenities of life while nominally confined in the Tower. Of the other prisoners who had chanced their luck in war, some made their peace with the king and served with him in Flanders in 1297, and some were probably ransomed.

general roll could, too, be adapted to the political interests of the patron, as Collins' Roll was tampered with in the Yorkist interest in the mid-fifteenth century. It might be expected that any thirteenth-century banneret would have a roll wherein he and his kinsmen figured, but almost all have disappeared.

The work in peace-time of the Edwardian heralds is known to us primarily through their association with tournaments which they proclaimed (or prohibited) and regulated under the marshal. Though scores of medieval tournaments can be dated, only one tournament roll of our period (Dunstable) survives. With one exception (Glover) the surviving lists do not seem to have been made expressly to suit the king, the prince, or the earls. It is likely that they were drawn up for the men whom Professor Powicke has appositely called Edward's 'Great Captains' —the professional soldiers of whom the more important were styled bannerets, such as Roger Mortimer (St. George), Robert Clifford (Caerlaverock and perhaps Collins), Reginald de Grey and Henry Percy (Falkirk). Of these men Percy is the only one known to have had a King of Arms in his retinue. Such documents are thought, from their contents, to have had their origins in the marches of Wales and Scotland and at Dover, and this explains the presence of Welsh, Scottish, and foreign coats of arms. The clues made use of may be paralleled in the paintings of the great Flemish period, for the man who has paid the minstrel or herald-painter appears somewhat to advantage by being better positioned upon the roll which he has commissioned, just as the donor not infrequently found a place in the picture presented by him to his church (cf. the well-known 'St. George and the donor' in Glasgow Art Gallery).

The earls bulk large in the political history of the age, as in the rolls of arms, but by and large they did not win or lose Edward's battles for him, or make their name in tournaments. Apart from Warwick and Gloucester it was

the Great Captains and the tournament-men such as Robert de Tony, the Swan Knight, or Richard de Argentine,
King of the Greensward in 1308 and later the hero of Bannockburn at the cost of his life, who were the popular
military figures of the age. Apart from their personal and
political importance the genealogical affiliations of the
earls are of far-reaching heraldic importance, and so most
rolls include a number of them, by title rather than by
family name.

There may be a clue to the origin of some of the general
rolls in the fact that the heralds, in order to live, had to
attach themselves to patrons. Their work was necessary,
but they had to be paid for it, and so throughout the century all but the most important heralds must also have
performed as minstrels. More will be said of this below.
From the heraldic point of view it is part of my theme that
Stephen of Penchester, for thirty years Constable of Dover
Castle (Dering Roll), Roger Mortimer (St. George's
Roll), the guardian of England during Edward's absence
on Crusade, Robert Clifford (Caerlaverock), and Henry
Percy (Falkirk Roll) employed their own heralds, examples
of whose work has in each case come down to us.

The general rolls have a characteristic common to many
types of medieval literary composition, in that their purpose is not declared in the first line. There must be in all
medieval fine writing, and indeed in many modern works,
a justification, a *benivolentiae captatio, exordium* or *arenga*,
to attract the interest of the audience or, if a roll is in
question, the viewer. Thus the *raison d'être* of a roll is not
always immediately apparent. As with a Papal Bull or
medieval chronicle, there is much that not everyone would
think relevant, inserted while the compiler is addressing
himself to his task and to the audience. This perhaps fanciful idea would explain why the name of the patron (if
I am right) is to be found some little way down the list—
after the earls, but high enough up to appear slightly out
of focus.

Painted rolls, such as the Dering Roll, could only be produced at leisure, probably in the castle where the patron
resided or had his headquarters—be it Dover, Wigmore,
or Berwick. Perhaps it was this that led to the inclusion of
the coats of the more distinguished prisoners, honourably
confined until the arrival of their ransom-money. The
PRA could thus have been drawn up at Wallingford or
Berkhamsted, which were in the hands of Piers Gaveston
as Earl of Cornwall from 1307 to 1312, though our original copy of it has always been associated with the Northern
province, the great number of copies and partial copies
made in the succeeding centuries suggest a multiple
origin.

The history of our subject is much complicated by the
persistent efforts of heralds at all dates to produce facsimile copies of their treasures. This idiosyncrasy, which
is not due to any desire to deceive, is first noticed in the
Dering Roll, written c. 1278 in a hand that might have
been fashionable in the middle of the century. The habit is
rife in the fifteenth century, when the conscientious glos-
sator of the PRA betrays the date at which he is writing by
the nature of the ink in which his careful and accurate
additions are written. The same practice is obvious in
Charles' Roll, which as we have it is a good fifteenth-
century attempt, perhaps by a Welsh scribe, at a facsimile
copy of a thirteenth-century original. The habit persisted
with Dugdale,[1] who also adopted it in the famous 'Book
of Seals', now happily in print,[2] and it has something in
common with the 'frozen' scripts that persisted for so long
as Court Hands.

Rolls were not, I think, tampered with for genealogical
reasons before the fifteenth century. On the other hand
pride of ancestry or of great connexions led to the inclusion

[1] Dugdale deliberately formed his 'special hand' in 1635–7. See 'Sir Hilary
Jenkinson on the Handwriting of Sir William Dugdale', by Sir Anthony Wagner,
in the *Journal of the Society of Archivists*, vol. ii, no. 4 (October 1961), p. 163.
[2] *Sir Christopher Hatton's 'Book of Seals'*, edited in 1950 for the Northamptonshire Record Society by the late Lewis C. Loyd and Doris Mary Stenton (no. 94).

of some fabulous persons, and many deceased worthies, in otherwise genuine lists. It is not easy to generalize about this, for, apart from the Occasional rolls, most medieval Rolls of Arms suffer from the defect that, as Greenstreet somewhere remarked, they are *retrospective* in character.

So the handwriting of these rolls is not always a safe guide to their date. The Dering Roll in its present form cannot have been begun before *c.* 1278, but it is written throughout in a hand that was fashionable about thirty years earlier.[1] This might, of course, be the hand of a very old man writing as he had been taught to write in his youth.[2] It is much more likely to be a deliberate archaism; and may be even later than the date (*c.* 1278) demanded by the internal evidence. It is a hand that fits the *floruit* of No. 1 upon the Roll, Richard Fitz Roy, or Richard de Warenne (b. about 1195, d. after May 1242),[3] lord of Chilham in Kent, a bastard son of King John, who married Rohese of Dover.

A roll such as the Dering Roll may be closely connected with a Castle-guard roll drawn up by a feodary or bailiff of fees. This helps to explain some of the anomalies, for it is a desperate feature of all feodaries or rentals, as all local historians are aware, that old lists are made to serve the rent-collector by changing only a few of 'the Occupiers' from time to time or, as with our copy of the PRA, bringing it up to date by deleting a label here and there. All great people had their 'feodaries' or bailiffs of fees in the middle ages, and they were usually appointed for a county or group of counties. The Dering Roll is not quite a rental or feodary of Dover Castle and the fees appurtenant, but it is probably based upon one. Later, especially perhaps Lancastrian or Tudor, interpolations are done for a purpose,

---

[1] Cf. N. R. Ker, 'The Date of the "Tremulous" Worcester Hand', in *Leeds Studies in English and Kindred Languages* (1937), pp. 28–29.

[2] See *CEMRA*, Plate II, where the caption *c.* 1300 suggests that this is a copy: *c.* 1270–80 is suggested as the date of composition.

[3] *R. lit. cl.* 215[b], Matt. Par., *Chron. Maj.*, iv, pp. 491–2, but read *filius Regis* for *filius Rogeri*.

to assist in falsifying a genealogy and so to glorify a name and pander to family pride. This happened unfortunately to the Dering Roll while it was in the possession of Sir Edward Dering.

The rolls to some extent betray their origin by their contents, and can thus be localized, even if they appear to be general rolls. The PRA is remarkable in attempting a distinct list of the bannerets not long after the death of Edward I. It is also the only one that is truly national, for it excludes foreigners. Most of the others contain Welsh, Gascon, or Scottish gentlemen at court as stipendiary knights, and some Welshmen numbered among the recipients of knighthood at the Feast of the Swans in 1306 are not included, e.g. Griffin de la Pole, Morgan ap Meredith, Hugh Howel, and Badham alias ap Adam. The PRA bears the stamp of authority and can only have been completed at or near the habitat of the royal heralds; possibly, in view of the date, at one of Piers Gaveston's castles; or, if Edward II was personally interested (which may be doubted), at Windsor. This suggestion is based upon the hypothesis that the plan, probably initiated by Edward I, was in fact set on foot if not carried to completion during Gaveston's regency. It accords with all that we know of the man.

At the battle of 'Fawkirk' (1298), as at the sieges of Caerlaverock (July 1300) and Stirling (30 May 1304), the Rolls of Arms show that two-thirds of the bannerets of England were present. It is shown—and not, I think, elsewhere—that at Falkirk the fourth brigade was led by Warenne. The rolls show, too, that the number of fighting men employed was substantially the same in all three actions. This is cited as an example of the value of such rolls to the military historian. It is from the heralds, too, as attested by the chronicler Trivet, that we know that there were about a thousand knights in London in May 1306 for the Feast of the Swans.

In a more general way the rolls reveal sociological

trends not easily observable in narrative sources. It is for example very noticeable that when 'the main chance' seems to be disappearing on the Welsh border, Clifford, Percy, and Warwick find greater scope for their ambitions in the north, and establish themselves on a permanent footing at Appelby, Alnwick, and Castle Barnard.

For the genealogist even the best of the rolls has its limitations. The PRA includes—or retains—at the head of the list of bannerets, the name of John Wake of Liddell, a large Cumberland barony. The herald is a better authority on his coat of arms than on the date of his death. For the PRA appears to be a roll of persons supposed to be living at the date of composition, which was after, but not long after, 1308. But John Wake died in 1300. Since the heralds' business is with the rightful ownership of correctly blazoned coats, no great harm is done, heraldically speaking. But this is a roll that Sir William Dugdale, herald and antiquary, had learned to trust, and if it includes John Wake he will follow it against the evidence of the Chancery records, which show that there was no John in the Wake succession in 1308/9. So, against the evidence available to him in the 'escheats' or inquisitions *post mortem*, Dugdale in his *Baronage* tells us that John Wake *had an heir John, who did not live very long*—but long enough, he means, to be inserted in the PRA. For John he should have read (and the roll should read if it is to be kept up to date as of 1308/9) Thomas, though Thomas was only about ten when the roll was compiled.[1]

The principles upon which the rolls were compiled is not at all obvious. The Dering Roll, for example, emanating it is believed from Dover Castle, contains a high proportion of officials (e.g. fifteen sheriffs of Kent or Sussex), tenants-in-chief, and families closely connected with the royal court. But this is only incidental: these men are not listed because they are tenants-in-chief or officials

[1] Dugdale, *Baronage* (1675), *s.v.* Wake. Collins' Roll, which depends on fifteenth-century copies, naturally abounds in this kind of error.

or because they lived in Kent or Sussex. A feudal or functional link is likely in a roll of arms of the thirteenth century.

This was the great age of heraldry in Britain, but heralds did not draw up lengthy and expensive painted rolls for their own amusement. They could not work *in vacuo*. They, like the minstrels from whose ranks they were just emerging, could exercise their profession only if they could find a patron. To be a private or baronial herald in the thirteenth century can hardly have been a full-time occupation. The combination with minstrelsy was as old as heraldry itself and lasted throughout our period. Heraldry was an essential matter in the thirteenth century, but not every great lord, we may suppose, was fond of minstrelsy. In every age and country some men are tone-deaf. We do not know, for example, that Simon de Montfort maintained any paid minstrels, but someone had to be, and was, at hand before the battle of Evesham *qui expertus erat in cognitione armorum*—in this instance, Nicholas his barber.

The expertise involved in the recognition of coats of arms and their description necessitated the presence of heralds at tournaments, sieges, battles or Round Tables, or wherever organized forces were employed. They were there to assist the Marshals, and sometimes—but how often?—to compile a list of those present. It is only rarely that such a list survives. These are the Occasional Rolls—Falkirk, Caerlaverock, Galloway, Stirling, Dunstable, and the Nativity Roll.

But there are a number of thirteenth-century rolls whose original purpose is not at all clear, and it is of these that it seems reasonable to inquire who commissioned them or paid for them to be made. A roll of 300 to 600 names with painted shields of arms is not made out of sheer *joie de vivre*. The work was highly technical: it demanded knowledge, skill, and leisure and the kind of resources hardly to be found in thirteenth-century England outside a royal palace, a monastery, or a baronial castle. The example of Matthew Paris—our only monkish herald-painter—suffices to show what a great Benedictine monastery could produce, but no 'Rolls' in roll form are associated with monasteries. The royal heralds would find accommodation enough while Henry III or Edward I was on the throne, and the baronial herald must be supposed to have had his headquarters in one of his lord's castles. Painted rolls presuppose the equivalent of a monastic scriptorium in which to work.

Baronial life, and hence that of the herald or minstrel, centred on the castle. The minstrel and the 'harpur' perform there and are a part of its life, in reality no less than in romance. It is the economic and administrative as well as military centre of its district. Where else should the herald find and (as minstrel) entertain his patron? For this reason it may be thought likely that the *Song of Caerlaverock* was composed in the Castle of Caerlaverock, in honour of Clifford, who became Constable of the Castle when the siege was over. The Dering Roll was, we may now say with some confidence, made at Dover. St. George's Roll, if the same line of thought is followed, might tentatively be assigned to Wigmore, and Glover's Roll to Kenilworth. The Falkirk Roll with the Nativity Roll endorsed is, I take it, Walter le Rey's Roll from Henry Percy's headquarters in Northumberland, but not yet Alnwick.[1] Collins' Roll is most likely to have been made at Berwick, or near by.

[1] It could of course be Topclive, but that is a long way south from Falkirk. Some border castle is clearly indicated, if the roll ever existed in a painted form, but this I doubt. As a blazoned roll, in its present form it could have been made in camp and copied anywhere.

II

THE EDWARDIAN CAVALRY

(i) KNIGHTS BACHELOR

THE contractual method of raising any army has two
aspects. There are the contracts made by the king
with his magnates and the sub-contracts made by
the magnates with their retainers. The former can be
illustrated by the agreement between the king and certain
earls and bannerets for the Falkirk campaign,[1] and the
various indentures between Clifford and the king.[2] The
more detailed sub-contracts are almost as scarce, and come
to light about the same time.[3] It was the wars on the Scottish border that gave impetus to this system and helped
to fill such a roll as Collins' with knights who came from all
parts of England as retainers, not necessarily tenants. This
and the mobility of ambitious and usually anonymous
heralds makes the localization of a general roll of arms a
hazardous matter.

The information provided by the few surviving contracts is of great value, but the composition of Edwardian
armies will always be quite incomplete. Whether a baron
is doing feudal service or serving by contract it is unusual
to know the make-up of his retinue, except as to the numbers he brought with him. This is one of the reasons for
the high value here set upon the Falkirk Roll,[4] because it
has been printed side by side with the horse-inventories of
the campaign, both from the king's household and others,
thus enabling us to examine the personnel of many of the
troops led by bannerets. These retinues were, even in the

---

[1] *Infra*, p. 104.   [2] *Infra*, p. 99 (A.D. 1296).   [3] *Infra*, pp. 141–2.
[4] *Infra*, pp. 103–11.

reign of Henry III, clad in the livery of the baron or earl who led them. All private officials or servants great and small wore 'robes' provided by their masters. A remarkable instance was brought to light by Lady Stenton of a north-country robber who in 1218 bought a hundred marks' worth of cloth to clothe his following of fifteen men 'as if he had been a baron or an earl'.[1] It is an intriguing question whether those who had been knighted by the king in person in 1306 wore any distinguishing mark. Their 'robes' had been supplied by the king, yet many of them in 1309 at the tournament of Dunstable are found in the retinues of other lords. It seems that the king bene-fited only quite indirectly from knighting men in person. They did not *ipso facto* become king's knights, though a few were admitted into the royal household.

In January 1296 there was an inquiry into the number of persons worth £40 a year in land, as well knights as others, to ensure that they were provided with horses and arms for the defence of the realm,[2] and in November of the same year all £20 freeholders were to be distrained to become knights.[3] So in summoning 900 men by name in 1301 the King was not acting in the dark. He had recent information about those bound by the Assize of Arms and the Statute of Winchester (1285) to obey his summons, and the so-called *Statutum de Militibus* of 1278 had provided for those who could be exempted and those who could not.

This summons in 1301 by individual writ to 900 of the country gentry was issued during the parliament of Lin-coln.[4] In this Edward pursued the old policy of 'distraint of knighthood' to its logical conclusion. All £40 free-holders were ordered to attend the king with horses and arms to Scotland. And there the story ends.[5] For we are

---

[1] Cited by Professor Helen Cam in *History*, December 1940, p. 224, from Lady Stenton's *Eyre of York* (Selden Soc.), p. 424.
[2] *Parl. Writs*, i. 278 (13 January 1296).   [3] Ibid., p. 280.
[4] Ibid., pp. 349–56 (summons of 12 March 1301 for Berwick, 24 June 1301).
[5] F. M. Powicke, *The Thirteenth Century*, pp. 693–4; Ramsay, *Dawn of the Constitution*, p. 480.

not told how many of those summoned were already knights, or how many of them actually came, or even what those latter did when they arrived. Nor do we know how many of those liable to go sent two sergeants instead of a knight.[1]

This method of individual summons had the advantage of catching in the net men who ought to have assumed knighthood and had not, as the Chief Constable of Kesteven, Geoffrey de Bounne (or Bourne), who held fragments of fees here and there so that his total holdings made him liable to distraint at the figure named. He did in fact become a knight.[2] The wording of the writ—they are asked (*rogati*) not ordered to come—shows that the basis of political obligation was not easily definable. It is not feasible at the moment to say how many of these 900 men were gentlemen of coat-armour, but since they were serving *ad vadia nostra* from 24 July 1301 it is not impossible that a horse-inventory will yet be found to tell us more about their status.

The writ of 1301 appears to be the only occasion when the policy of distraint at the £40 level was put into action. No articulate opposition is heard of, or any defence on the ground of overriding necessity or the common need, or even the Statute of Winchester. Possibly this list should be compared with the 941 knights of the PRA, though the two records are a decade apart, and at the date of the latter a list of about 1,250 knights can be compiled.[3]

The scarcity of knights was due not simply to a distaste for military service, but to economic and social changes. In the twelfth century arms and equipment might have

---

[1] Cf. Powicke, op. cit., pp. 116, 141, for a similar attempt in 1254 to muster all £20 freeholders, owing to a threat of war with Spain, which abated on the marriage of the Lord Edward to Eleanor of Castile.

[2] See *A Lincolnshire Assize Roll of 1298*, edited as vol. 36 (1944) for the Linc. Rec. Soc. by the late W. S. Thomson.

[3] This estimate is from my own card-index of the Occasional rolls of arms, members of parliament, and sheriffs. I have not yet controlled it by Dr. E. C. Moor's much more extensive survey.

cost only £5 or 20 marks,[1] but the development of complete body armour for man and horse, together with a war-horse strong enough to bear such a weight, increased the cost from five- to ten-fold. A good Edwardian *dextrarius* alone would fetch from £20 to £100—perhaps equivalent to the cost of a light tank in 1939. Moreover the Earl Marshal was entitled to a palfrey when a tenant-in-chief was knighted or did homage.[2] The lord could take, however, an aid *pur faire fils chevalier* to recover part of his outlay.

It may be that the increase in the civil duties of a knight acted as an even more potent deterrent than the purely economic factors. For once a man had been knighted he could be called upon to act as coroner, or as a juryman on a Grand Assize, as a knight of the shire if elected, or as a chief constable of his hundred. For these reasons there was a steady flow of respites of knighthood, by which a man was excused for one year or a term of years, or for life, for a sum of money that varied according to the needs of the Crown and according to the stipulated term or the age of the tenant. The conditions of exemption for tenants on ancient demesne and burgage tenants were laid down in the *Statutum de Militibus* of 26 June 1278.[3]

There are literary allusions to bachelors, that is knights bachelor, from the time of William the Marshal, but they do not occur much in public records until the middle of the century. An early example is Thomas Malesmains, to be retained as one of King John's bachelors at £60 per annum payable from the Chamber, until he be provided with £60 worth of land.[4] From the middle of the century they are not infrequent. Sir Robert le Chambe[r]leyn,

---

[1] *Pipe Roll 14 Henry II*, pp. 21, 113, &c.

[2] *Fleta*, bk. II, cap. 5.

[3] For this statute, which used to be dated 1 Ed. II, see *Stat. of the Realm*, i. 229. On the whole subject see the comprehensive but neglected paper by F. M. Nicholls in *Archaeologia*, vol. 39 (1863), pp. 189–244, 'On Feudal and Obligatory Knighthood'.

[4] *Rot. lit. pat.* i. 190ᵇ–191ᵃ (14 July 1216).

bachelor of Sir Philip Basset, sent 'his best and favourite esquire, William de Keleshale, to the battle of Evesham with horses and arms'.[1] From this time the word occurs more frequently. In 1262 the Wardrobe was told to let the household bachelors and king's sergeants-at-arms have their usual robes.[2] On 20 October that year the king sent word from France that all *the king's bachelors* who held counties (i.e. as sheriffs) were to keep them until his arrival in England, and in 1263 the King wrote 'to all his bachelors at Hereford'.[3] At a date not long before this, probably as late as 1262, the Lord Edward was spoken of as a bachelor.[4] The Earl of Gloucester's bachelors in June 1267—the date of his march on London—are mentioned on the Patent roll. But there are still no bannerets in official records.

Though the approximate numbers of both bachelors and bannerets in Edwardian armies can be discovered, the number of 'troopers' is much more uncertain, for the subject is bedevilled by a fluctuating terminology. The usage of the royal household does not define or reflect social status in the outside world,[5] and each class of government records—or perhaps only each government department—has its own conventions. The *valletti* of the Marshalsea rolls, who are translated into 'yeomen' in Public Record Office calendars, are in common parlance the esquires of the knights and barons of Edward I or of the royal household itself.[6] In other royal records persons of the same standing as esquires are called *scutiferi*, sometimes

---

[1] *Misc. Inq.* i. 932. The style is—or was to the editor in 1916—so unusual that 'Bachilar' is cross-referenced in the Index of Subjects under 'Language, curiosities of'.

[2] *Close Rolls* (November 1263), pp. 163, 166.

[3] *Close Rolls* (1263), p. 274 and pp. 269–73 *passim*.

[4] *PQW* (Salop), pp. 679–80, 682ª, and cf. *s.v.* Kent.

[5] Notes on this matter will be found in Taswell-Langmead, *English Const. History*, ed. T. F. Plucknett (1946), pp. 226–7, and *The Tournament in the Thirteenth Century*, p. 262 and refs., by the present author.

[6] In the *Liber Quotidianus Contrarotularius Garderobe* of 28 Ed. I (Soc. of Antiquaries, 1787) *Scutiferi* in the text are called *Valetti* in the margin (p. 232).

armigeri. These men, together with the *servientes ad arma* or sergeants (from whom they were usually distinguished by birth), are usually styled 'troopers', or men-at-arms, by modern historians. All were paid a shilling a day and many of them would become knights. The chroniclers call them *homines ad arma* or *armati*, when at this period they fought side by side as heavy cavalry. But in the fourteenth century *armati* is technically confined to light cavalry. The *eques coopertus* of the heavy cavalry had a skirting of chain mail over a linen covering.[1]

(II) BANNERS AND BANNERETS

In the Falkirk inventories it is usually stated if a man is a knight. If he is *Dominus* with other knights in his retinue he may be counted as a *strenuus* banneret. Other *Domini* are high accounting officials (usually of the wardrobe) and may be beneficed clerks, though not necessarily with cure of souls.

The use of the banneret's banner is technically important. To ride *with banners displayed* was a sign of open war: it might be in levying war against the king in his realm. This was a breach of the feudal contract between lord and vassal, and later a token of treason to a sovereign prince. This use of the banner is a link between the rebellion of the young Earl Marshal in 1233, when he raised his standard at Woodstock,[2] and the later treason cases examined by Mr. M. H. Keen.[3] It was one of the accusations levied against William Wallace in 1306 and Roger Damory in 1322. Here the jurisdiction of the later Court of Chivalry (though it is not so styled) is seen, acting in 1322 under the Constable and Marshal and styled in the

---

[1] Morris, *Welsh Wars*, p. 53, from PRO Misc. Acct. Roll of 1277 (Exch. Accts. 3/15).

[2] *Richard of Cornwall*, by N. Denholm-Young, pp. 24–28, and Wendover in Matt. Par., *Chron. Maj.* iii. 248. Cf. *Close Rolls* (1233), 253, 257, 258.

[3] *T. R. Hist. Soc.* (1962), pp. 85–103, 'Treason under the Law of Arms', pp. 85–103, especially pp. 93–94, 102.

Roll *Placita Exercitus*. Sir Adam Banastre, who made a sworn confederacy with other knights (8 October 1315) and vainly attacked Liverpool (23 October), provides another instance, for he stole the King's standard and displayed it at Manchester.[1]

The knight bachelor and the knight banneret had the same coat of arms, but the distinction in rank—for the banneret was paid double and led a troop—was marked by the use of a pennant by the bachelor and a rectangular banner by the banneret. In the later (e.g. *c.* 1340 Cooke's Ordinary) Rolls of Arms it was convenient to display a banner for a banneret and a shield for a 'simple knight'.[2] The thirteenth-century Rolls of Arms do not distinguish bachelors from bannerets. Froissart, in a famous passage, explains how it was only necessary to snip off the tail of a bachelor's pennant—he is describing the promotion of Chandos—to make a banner. The feasibility of this operation clearly depends upon the disposition of the charge upon the pennant, unless it is to suffer mutilation in the process. However, the distinction is purely military and the coat of arms is not altered on promotion.

Morris[3] thought that a son of a baron was 'by prescriptive right' a banneret, but this is not so, as the story of Brian Fitz Alan[4] and the Wardenship of Scotland plainly shows. Fitz Alan was made Warden and remained a bachelor, although possessed of the barony of Bedale, a very poor one. He explained that he could not afford to lead a troop, which was incumbent upon a banneret. It was not a question of land to support his dignity, but money to pay his men.

---

[1] *Vita Edwardi Secundi*, ed. N. Denholm-Young, p. 64.

[2] The bachelor is called *miles simplex* from 1298 (Falkirk Roll) at least, but not yet so styled by some departments of the king's household.

[3] *Welsh Wars of Edward I*, i. 71.

[4] Sir Brian Fitz Alan's copy of *Perlesvaus* (a mutilated form of *Perceval*) is now MS. Hatton 82 (see fol. 5) in the Bodleian Library (*Sum. Catal.*, no. 4092). See Plate 15 in my *Handwriting in England and Wales* (Cardiff, 1954). For 'Le beau Brian Fitz Aleyn' and his quarrel with Hugh Pointz, who bore the same arms, see Wagner, *Heralds and Heraldry*, pp. 18–19, 120.

The pennon or *guidon* existed in more than one form. The lance-flag represented in the Luttrell Psalter, a manuscript made for Sir Geoffrey Luttrell (*fl.* 1310–20), a Lincolnshire knight bachelor (no. 645 in the PRA), is a triangular flag that could by no means be converted into a banner without mutilating the arms. The knight bachelor's *guidon* envisaged by Froissart in his story of the promotion in 1369 of Sir John Chandos on the field of Navaretta by the Black Prince can only have been a forked or many-tailed flag, the tails bearing no charge. The Chandos arms were a red lion with a forked tail on a gold field.[1] Sir John presented his pennon reversed in his hand to the Prince, explaining that he had sufficient lands to support the rank of banneret, and the Prince 'cut off the tail to make the square and returning it to him by the handle said . . .'.[2]

Illustrations of banners are seen in the Douce Apocalypse of uncertain date, but between 1254 and 1272.[3] The distinction between banners for bannerets and shields for simple knights is found in Cooke's Ordinary of about A.D. 1340.[4]

The banner, used by king and knight, is repeatedly illustrated by Matthew Paris (before 1259). That of St. Louis bears the same charge as the shield, and the

---

[1] PRA, no. 951. Roger Chandos was in the Bohun retinue (no. 28) at the Dunstable tournament (see p. 125 *infra*) in 1309, as mentioned by Dugdale, *Baronage*, i. 503 with wrong date.

[2] This may be read in Seldon, *Titles of Honour*, p. 2, cap. 3, or in the epitomized Globe edition of Froissart, chap. iv, p. 102. Navaretta, or Najero, was an episode in an attempt to restore Pedro the Cruel to the throne of Castile, when Chandos overcame du Guesclin, the Constable of France, himself a bachelor on appointment as constable. This type of flag is repeatedly shown in the Bayeux Tapestry, and Mrs. Margaret Labarge kindly tells me that it is illustrated in the Maciejowski Bible (*c.* A.D. 1250), fol. 12*a*. This is MS. 638 in the Pierpont Morgan Library in New York.

[3] If one of the banners represented is to be taken as that of Simon de Montfort the date is likely to be 1265–72. See A. G. and W. O. Hassall, *The Douce Apocalypse* (1962). The editors think that the manuscript is a product of the Court school of painting at Westminster.

[4] See *CEMRA*, Plate V,

lance and banner reversed are used to commemorate the deed.

(iii) CREATION OF KNIGHTS

A man could be knighted at any age.[1] The higher his social status the more likely he was to be made a knight while still only a boy: Henry III was nine, Edward I fifteen, and Gilbert de Clare sixteen. It was clearly desirable that he should at least be able to ride a horse. But the ceremony, which had nothing to do with the succession to landed property, might take place at any age. Edmund of Cornwall was twenty-two when he was knighted on 13 October 1272 with fifty English and foreign nobles by Henry III at Westminster, and Edward of Caernarvon was about the same age in 1306.

The habit of holding investitures, or mass-knightings, obtained throughout the century. In 1241 the king knighted Peter of Savoy and fifteen others in Westminster Abbey on St. Edward's Day (13 October), the feast that he always celebrated with great solemnity.[2] On the occasion of the marriage on 26 December 1251 at York of the King of Scots with Henry's daughter Margaret, twenty young men were knighted. We are asked to believe that a thousand English knights and sixty Scottish ones were present.[3] On 13 October 1261 the king knighted his new son-in-law John of Brittany, and the Lord Edward Henry and Simon, the sons of Simon de Montfort. A total of eighty young men were knighted on this occasion.[4] There may have been something like a parallel to the Feast of the Swans (1306) when Henry III on 30 August 1254 *summoned* all his tenants-in-chief not being knights, and *invited* tenants of other lords, for love of his son Edward, to be knighted with the Lord Edward by Alfonso

---

[1] See Plucknett, *Legislation of Edward I*, p. 78, for the financial implications of Westm. I, cap. 36 (1275), which discouraged knighting before the age of fifteen.
[2] Matt. Par., *Chron. Maj.*, iv. 85–86.   [3] Op. cit., p. 268.   [4] *Flores*, ii. 456.

of Castile.[1] But, unlike the later occasion, there is no record of how many were present.[2]

The creation of knights by the king continued sporadically throughout the year and is recorded in the chancery records, under writs of privy seal for the issue of robes. Horses and armour were not provided. One such bundle of writs has survived for the period 20 November 1305 to 20 November 1306,[3] that is just before and just after the great Feast of the Swans in May 1306, which has been fully discussed in another place.[4] The admissions of knights to the royal household were registered individually year by year in the Wardrobe accounts, of which Droxford's book (extending to 424 pages) has survived for our period.[5]

The privy seal writs just cited give valuable details of the robes to be supplied, and a few other documents are of assistance for an earlier period. The robes varied according to the social status of the recipient, and whether he was a bachelor (*miles simplex* at this period) or a banneret. Sometimes the fur is specified, but more often it is to be 'according to his rank'.

The cloth from which the knights could have their robes made up was issued from the Great Wardrobe in lengths.[6] It may be useful to note that a robe (like a *villa integra*) meant more than might be suspected, for it included a *tunic, supertunic, pallium,* and *capa*.[7] Robes for an

---

[1] *Close Rolls* (1253–4), 30 August, pp. 153–4.

[2] Sir Maurice Powicke states that the king's letters reached the chancellor too late to be acted on (*The Thirteenth Century*, p. 548). For the knighting of Edward see *Fl. Wig. Cont.*, p. 185, Matt. Par. v. 450, and *Foed.* i. 528.

[3] PRO E.101/369/4, a P.S. file.

[4] The 'Swan list' was copied, though not directly, from the PRO list in E. 101/362/20 (a document joined chancery fashion and written on one side only of the parchment) by Elias Ashmole into his *History and Institution of the Order of the Garter* (1672), pp. 38–39, and used by Dugdale in his *Baronage* (*passim*). See my paper cited *infra*, p. 49 n. 3.

[5] PRO E. 101/369/11 (36 Ed. I).

[6] Robes for 26 persons knighted with the Prince in 1306 are specified in PRO C. 47/3/30.

[7] *Cl. R.* (1244), p. 269, (1245), p. 309, (1246), p. 493, (1247), p. 530: knights ought to have squirrels' fur not rabbits' skin (1253). Cited by A. E. Stamp,

ordinary knight cost about £1 in the first half of the century, but a magnate would spend £9.[1]

The chargers that they rode might come from Flanders, Italy, or Spain. They were ridden on a single rein with a very severe bit giving tremendous leverage, with box or cowboy (Texas) saddles as still used by the *gardiens* of the wild cattle in the Camargue in southern France. The spurs were heavily rowelled. The rider mounted in the modern, not the 'classical', way, i.e. he faced the animal's tail, holding the saddle and reins, while the groom held down the stirrup-leather on the off-side.[2]

The right of creating knights had in the twelfth century been much more widely exercised and until the end of the middle ages the practice lingered on of one knight creating another. Becket when Chancellor had knighted the young noblemen whom he had brought up in his household.[3] William Marshal was knighted by the Chamberlain of Tancarville,[4] and he in turn knighted 'the young Henry', son of Henry II.[5] A king of Scotland in the thirteenth century claimed that he could have been knighted by any catholic prince or by any of his nobles.[6] Richard de Clare, Earl of Gloucester, in 1250 knighted William de Wilton and Peter le Botiler at Hanley Castle.[7] Simon de Montfort, Earl of Leicester, knighted Gilbert de Clare and his brother Thomas de Clare, with Robert de Vere, Earl of Oxford, before the battle of Lewes.[8] Warenne, Earl of Surrey, created new knights before the battle of Stirling Bridge on 10 September 1297.[9]

'Court and Chancery of Henry III', in *Essays presented to James Tait*, pp. 310–11.

[1] *R. lit. cl.*, p. 471, &c. Theodoric le Tyes' cost £9 in 1205 (ibid., p. 56).

[2] *Illustrations to the Life of St. Alban*, ed. E. A. Lowe, E. F. Jacob, and M. R. James (1924) for the Roxburghe Club.

[3] F. M. Nicholls, op. cit.

[4] S. Painter, *William the Marshal*, p. 20.   [5] Ibid., p. 36.

[6] Matt. Par., *Chron. Maj.*, v, pp. 267–9.

[7] *Ann. Theok.*, p. 142.

[8] Ramsay, *Dawn of the Constitution* (1908), p. 222 and refs.

[9] Hemingburgh (Eng. Hist. Soc.), p. 136.

But it was always an especial honour to be knighted by the king himself. From time to time he invested foreigners, as at Whitsuntide 1251 when Henry III knighted James, nephew of Mr. Marino, the papal vice-chancellor.[1] Of the greatest of medieval royal investitures, before and after the Feast of the Swans (i.e. May 1306 and February 1307), I have written elsewhere,[2] and the results of the inquiries made at that time are called in evidence throughout this book. Perhaps the most important point that here arises in the theory of knighthood is that such investitures were part of the process by which the king gradually arrogated to himself alone the right of creation.

Before the investiture, and before the aspirant's vigil in church, he should, according to a persistent theory of chivalrous behaviour, have taken a ceremonial bath. Not a trace of evidence for this has been found in the thirteenth century, but Geoffrey of Anjou is said to have bathed before being knighted in 1180.[3] The essential feature, as described by Matthew Paris, is always girding with the sword-belt (*baltheo militari*) and the assumption of gilt spurs—hence the later *eques auratus*. An 'Order of Knighthood of the Bath' is mentioned in the sentence of degradation pronounced upon Sir Ralph Grey by John Tiptoft, Earl of Worcester, the Constable, in 1464.[4] The present Order of the Bath is said to have been established in 1725 as a pretended revival of an order supposed to have been created by Henry IV at his coronation in 1399.[5] Yet the lack of evidence for the thirteenth century did not deter Dugdale in his *Baronage*, under Basset of Drayton[6] and in at least twenty other instances referring to the

---

[1] *Cl. R.* (1247–51), p. 450.   [2] *Vide infra*, p. 49 n. 3.

[3] *Recueil des Historiens de la France*, tome XII, p. 521.

[4] The sentence upon Grey is cited at length by Mr. M. H. Keen, op. cit., pp. 90–91, from *Warkworth's Chronicle*, ed. J. O. Halliwell, pp. 36–39 notes, in *Camden Soc.*, Old Ser., x (1839).

[5] *Enc. Brit.*, art. 'Chivalry', by G. G. C[oulton]. Some absurdities are repeated in this pleasantly readable article.

[6] W. Dugdale, *Baronage*, i. 379.

Feast of the Swans, from describing the creation as 'by *Bathing* with the *Prince* and other Ceremonies'. What Dugdale really meant may be left to the imagination, but at times of mass knighting or investitures on the field of battle the ceremonial bath is clearly impracticable. 'Dubbing' with the sword was probably universally recognized as the essential preliminary.

(IV) KING'S KNIGHTS: *COMMILITONES*

a. King's Knights

A class apart is formed by the king's knights and king's bannerets, who receive robes from the king's household, or a fee in lieu thereof. These men are the leaders of the household cavalry. They formed the fourth brigade at Falkirk. Some of them are the king's personal bodyguard, but they are also the constables of his castles[1] and his trusted officials in those positions where soldiers rather than clerks were required. Their importance is sometimes obscured by classing them with the distinguished foreigners and other persons who were given 'money fiefs'; or with retaining fees in lieu of lands, or financial help to younger sons, or temporary payments to landed men.[2] The king's knights and king's bannerets are elusive people, for two reasons. Only a proportion of them, those who receive 'robes' and *bouche à court*, are named upon the annual household rolls, while those 'on location' or residing elsewhere are not so named because they are paid from some other possibly local source, for the Christmas term or the Easter term or both. Secondly, unlike the king's clerks or even king's yeomen, who are always so styled and very plentiful in the thirteenth-century Calendars of Close and Patent Rolls,

---

[1] S. Painter, *King John*, p. 352, has counted 72 royal, 14 episcopal, and 123 baronial castles.

[2] A useful conspectus of much scattered information has been made by Bruce D. Lyon, 'The Money Fief under the English Kings', in *EHR*, lxvi (1951).

the king's knights are nowhere indexed and hardly ever so styled. Yet they are the king's intimates and can be addressed by him in the second person, as was Paulinus Poever or Piper.[1] The peculiarly intimate relationship of the king's knights to the king is also expressed in the conditions of service. They are mentioned occasionally in the early Close Rolls, e.g. there is a letter from King John to Geoffrey Luttrell informing him that he was to receive his liveries *sicut alii milites de familia nostra recipiunt*,[2] but as at other dates these men only come to light incidentally, and usually in connexion with such payments. In the earliest surviving Wardrobe account the statement is 'in feodis militum annuis feoffetorum *quamdiu regi placuerit*'. On these knights, together with gifts to knights and liveries to sergeants-at-arms, the expenditure was £1,085. 1*s.* 4½*d.* in 1225, £631. 15*s.* 10*d.* in 1226, and £384. 4*s.* 9½*d.* in 1227.[3] This sudden drop is probably due to Richard of Cornwall's expedition to Gascony in these years, the cost of king's knights at home being reduced by the number of those on foreign service. More important than the amount of money involved is, for us, the statement, that does not recur, that the king's knights received their fees *quamdiu*. They were like the judges, royal stipendiaries, and received their fees (or *feoda*) and their robes as long as they behaved themselves.

After 1227 the king's knights disappear as a group from the Close Rolls. They were probably recorded in the Wardrobe books or rolls, but as these have not survived in bulk, the knights pass out of sight until towards the end of the century. No reference is made in these early Close Rolls to a distinction between bachelors and bannerets. Though bachelors are mentioned in literary and official

---

[1] Margaret Howell, *Regalian Right in Mediaeval England* (1962), p. 90, quotes a letter from Henry III to Paulinus Piper.

[2] *Rot. Norm.*, p. 54 (July 1202).

[3] T. F. Tout, *Chapters in English Administrative History*, i. 233. Seven king's knights were paid in 1217 and 1218, seventeen in 1219, and twenty-five in 1220 (*R. lit. cl.*, pp. 345, 362, 409, 444).

sources, bannerets nowhere occur. They are first mentioned allusively by Matthew Paris (who was writing up
his *Chronica Majora* from year to year) under A.D. 1240,
where in a marginal note are given the names of seven
vexilla ferentes with Earl Richard of Cornwall in 1240
and ten with Earl Simon de Montfort on the same expedition to the Holy Land,[1] and retrospectively as *vexilliferi* in
chronicles descriptive of the Barons' Wars but written
years later. About the middle of the century the phrase
'his [i.e. the king's] knight' is occasionally found, but no
special status is discoverable.

The thirteenth-century king's knights appear most
fully in the unprinted Wardrobe Rolls of 1285, 1286, and
1290 and the *Liber Quotidianus* of 1299–1300. Out of
twenty-three named as king's bannerets, seventeen were
barons, and a couple more may have been cadets of baronial
houses. Royalist families of long standing like Gray and
Daubeny are found.

The wages paid in addition to the robes were calculated
on a day-to-day basis.

b. Commilitones

The rolls of 1285, 1286, 1290, and these alone, list by
name among the household staff a sub-class of king's
knights headed *Commilitones*, a classical term for fellow
soldiers. The *commilitones* were paid at the same rate as
king's knights, i.e. 8 marks for a bachelor, 16 for a banneret. The bachelors like other king's knights are, from
time to time, promoted banneret. This apparently technical word *commilito* may conceal some development in the
organization of the household that failed to last. But some
of the *commilitones* bear names of baronial families that had
long been close to the throne. Possibly they comprised the
King's Troop, a *corps d'élite*. Certainly it looks as if,

---

[1] *Chron. Maj.* (R.S.), iv. 44. The two earls did not travel together. See my
Richard of Cornwall (1947), p. 41.

although 'fellow soldiers', they were 'more equal' than their fellows. The thirteenth century was a period of sworn associations and brotherhoods, and the official use of this word to denote a special group of king's knights may point to the intention of founding some confraternity or military order. The word in Edward I's reign is almost a vogue word,[1] quite possibly because of the king's use of it, and suggests the habit of admitting persons into religious confraternities, or the later (particularly French and German) custom of pacts of confraternity between individuals.[2]

c. Paulinus Piper

Paulinus Piper[3] may serve as an example of an educated knight, one of the *laici literati* who play an increasingly articulate part in the government of the country, both at Westminster and in the shires. Matthew Paris describes

---

[1] Edward I on crusade is made to say by Rishanger (p. 68, *s.a.* 1270), 'All my *commilitones* desert me.' In *Flor. Wig. Cont.* ii. 278 (A.D. 1295) Thomas Turberville, a king's knight, is described as fighting in Gascony *cum nonnullis sue militiae commilitonibus*. Again the word as used by Hem., p. 248, could mean 'knighted with', i.e. when Prince Edward left for Scotland in 1306 after the Feast of the Swans, he went *cum multis commilitonibus suis*. Cf. too *Ann. Lond., s.a.* 1265, p. 69.

[2] Cf. the German brotherhood rolls of the fifteenth century (*CEMRA*, p. xxxvi). Matt. Par., *Chron. Maj.* iii. 255, speaks of the *commilitones* of the young Earl Marshal.

[3] Matt. Par., v. 242. His arms were *scutum album flores de auro, reliqua rubea*. The name Piper represents the vernacular Peyvere, Peyre, Paverie, &c., of Bedfordshire, who bore the same or similar arms as the Peure, Peyfre, Peyforer, or Payforers of Kent. See Glover's Roll, the Dering Roll, and PRA Beds. and Kent. The latter held the sergeanty of the Fleet prison. Paulinus married a lady named Joan de Belhus, but the Belhus arms are not Bells or fleurs-de-lis but lioncels. There was and is a thirteenth-century inn at Lower Poever near Knutsford in Cheshire, on the Warenne fee, called the 'Bells of Poever alias the Warenne de Tabley'. I believe that there is here a canting allusion to the arms of the Poever family, particularly as Paulinus held one fee of the Warenne fee. But the symmetry of the story is broken by the intrusion of a recent tenant named Bell into the inn, and the inn is thought by the present licensee to have derived its name from him or his family. The inn was known by these names to Ormerod, the historian of Cheshire, and the origin of its name I leave to his successors, beyond pointing out that there was no armigerous family called Bell in the thirteenth century.

him as *miles literatus siue clericus militans*, who became Steward of the King's household. The ambiguity of status alluded to is equally apparent in the lives of the Stewards and Wardrobers fifty or sixty years later. Though one of the chief counsellors of Henry III until his death on 5 June 1251, Paulinus was a self-made man. He had started (probably on the Warenne fee and maybe in the earl's household) with scarcely two carucates of land. With-in a short time, says Paris, he had fifty. He was an insa-tiable buyer of lands and builder of manor-houses, as at 'Tuddington' in Bedfordshire, where he built a palace, with chapel, bedrooms, and other stone buildings covered with lead, complete with orchards and fish-ponds. Over many years it cost him five pounds or even ten marks in workmen's wages (? annually). When he died his heart was buried there, his body in London. He had taken the Cross in 1250.[1]

Paulinus is one of the inner circle of 'king's friends', to each of whom Matthew Paris applies the term *special counsellor*, or *principal counsellor*. He is said to have been thus appointed with the better-known John Mansel.[2] He was a king's knight, and his relatives followed the same career. On the household rolls, quoted above, for 1285 and 1286, Guy de la Pevere appears as a king's knight; Alexander de la Pevere as a banneret in 1285, not in 1286 (no doubt he was 'on a job'), but again in 1290. In 1303 another Paulinus Payvre and other distinguished royal servants, including Giles de Argentine, Mr. John Wal-wayn, Robert de Tony, Henry Segrave, Richard de Rokley, Thomas and William de Grey, broke into Mr. Peter de Dene's houses at Lawshall in Suffolk.[3] There is an un-pleasant air of fifteenth-century turbulence about this episode. As Steward of the Household Paulinus was head not only of the Wardrobe but of the other eight household

---

[1] Matt. Par. v. 101. For his possessions see Farrer, *Honours and Knight's Fees*, iii. 319, 434. *Cal. IPM Hen. III*, no. 453, relates to John Payvere.
[2] Matt. Par. iv. 294.   [3] *CPR* (1303), p. 86.

departments as well. In his day the Steward conducted much of the diplomatic work of the government, acting in some measure as a Foreign Secretary. He was in office for seven years—1244–51.[1]

King's knights were not invariably loyal. Allegiance to England as against Scotland or France was sometimes uncertain and wavering. Simon Fraser, a king's banneret at Falkirk (no. 9) and Caerlaverock (no. 54), deserted to the Scots in 1300. When he was captured and executed in 1306 his head was placed on London Bridge, with a fanfare of trumpets.[2]

d. The King's Knights at Sea

The best-known privateer of the thirteenth century is Henry Poun (alias Pechun, Pedene, Pethene, or Pezun), who was in 1265 in league with Simon de Montfort. The Countess of Leicester sent him several messages from Dover Castle in the first half of that year, and bought wine from him and his partners (*socii*).[3] He was captured and many of his associates killed by Edward's knights on 4 March 1266, shortly before the capitulation of Winchester to Roger Leybourne.[4] They are said to have received back all their 'liberties' on 24 March.[5] The date seems to fit in with the Earl of Gloucester's preparations

---

[1] Tout, *Chapters*, vi. 40.

[2] *Ann. Lond.* 148. Simon Fraser or Fresel was the eldest son of Simon Fraser, ancestor of the houses of Saltoun and Lovat. He had been captured at Dunbar in 1296 and only regained his liberty by swearing to serve Edward. Thus he appeared as a king's banneret at Falkirk in 1298 (no. 79 on the roll, he bore *Sable ov vj rosez dargent*). He was also at the siege of Caerlaverock in 1300 (no. 54), and in Collins' Roll his arms are given with a *label*, indicating that that entry was made before 1298. In 1299 he was paid as a king's banneret, but taken prisoner by the Scots, 4 September 1299 to 23 June 1300, and therefore not paid his fee for robes for that period.

[3] Botfield, op. cit., pp. 56, 63.

[4] *Ann. Wint.*, p. 104, and further 'Roger Leyburn and the Pacification of England, 1265–1267', by Alun Lewis, in *EHR*, liv (1939), 193–214.

[5] *Gerv. Cant.* ii. 244. Poun was condemned to 'honourable imprisonment with the expectation of the King's grace' (1 April 1266), through Gloucester's

for his rashly attempted *coup d'état* on London, to get better terms for the Disinherited. Poun had made the Isle of Wight his base, and Isabella de Fortibus, the Lady of the Isle, was forced to hand over the island to a royal Keeper of the Peace, for complicity in Poun's actions. This was in June 1267, but it was not for some years that Edward started negotiations for the purchase of the island, which he eventually secured for 6,000 marks in 1293.[1]

From isolated acts of piracy and reprisals the war at sea developed into a series of regular engagements. The course of these has caused much confusion. There were three sea battles off S. Mahé (1) against the Flemings in 1290, (2) against a coalition on 15 May 1293, and (3) a costly victory over the Normans on 26 May 1293. It was these battles that sparked off the war of 1295 over Gascony. In that year the picturesque rogue Sir Thomas Turberville, a king's knight, was trying in vain to persuade Edward to commit to him the guard of the coast.[2] This has nothing in common with the modern coastguard, but was a function of the fleet. It is also to be distinguished from the guard upon the coast undertaken by land forces organized by counties in 1264, 1295, and 1334–5, against the threat of foreign invasion.[3] These measures raised an early form of the question of Ship Money from inland as well as coastal towns. For in 1303 some ports refused to contribute to the expenses of the navy unless the adjacent towns were also made to pay.[4] The business of raising

intervention. This suggests that he was regarded as a gentleman, perhaps related to Nicholas Pesun, who bears *Ermine*, a fess *Azure* (? a lion rampant on the fess) as no. 45 on the Dering Roll of Arms.

[1] *CPR* (1266–72), pp. 142, 367, cf. 58, 86, 142, 572.

[2] See J. G. Edwards, 'The Treason of Thomas Turberville', in *Essays presented to F. M. Powicke* (Oxford, 1948), pp. 269–309.

[3] For Southampton see important documents in Goodman, *Chartulary of Winchester Cathedral*, nos. 354–5, 370. For the scare of 1334–5, see *Obedientiary Rolls of St. Swithin's, Winchester* (Hants Rec. Soc., 1892), ed. G. W. Kitchin, p. 243.

[4] *CPR* (2 March 1303), pp. 121 and 131 (for Cornwall).

ships, furnishing them with 'defensible men', and provisioning them for four months was entrusted in 1304 to the king's clerks.[1]

These *ad hoc* fleets helped to conquer Wales by cutting off supplies from Llewelyn. They assisted in the Scottish campaigns by transporting supplies to Scotland, and elsewhere by protecting merchant ships or even ports from attack; but most of all by transporting men, horses, and bullion in casks to Flanders or Gascony, as they had done throughout the century.

Amongst the king's household bachelors and bannerets are naturally to be found the admirals of his fleets, for naval warfare, in the absence of guns, inevitably consisted in boarding and capturing enemy ships, with the aid of archers and 'Greek fire' hurled from slings. Ships were largely used in transporting soldiers, so the king's stewards are prominent. William Charles was Captain over 'those of the shore of Norfolk and Suffolk' with the task of providing barges for the siege of Ely,[2] a good example of the Lord Edward's use of combined operations. This William Charles was steward of the royal household and had been sheriff of Essex. His son Sir Edward Charles was commissioned Admiral in 1306.[3] The Leyburns, too, are better known as king's knights, playing a considerable part in the general history of England, especially in Kent,[4] before William Leyburn was described in 1297 as Admiral of the Sea of the King of England and Captain of the Sea of the King of England.[5] The English Channel is described as *Mare Anglicanum* as early as 1278 and the much

---

[1] *Foed.*, pp. 961–2. Expenses of shipbuilding prior to Edmund of Lancaster's expedition of 1294 to Gascony, from 1 to 19 September, are found in Brit. Mus. Add. MS. 39947, cf. *Foed.* i. 808–9, &c.

[2] *CPR* (1267), pp. 44, 133.

[3] Ibid., pp. 493, 549.

[4] See 'Roger Leyburn and the Pacification of England, 1265–1267', by Alun Lewis, in *EHR* liv (1939), 193. In 1266 'all persons [are] to receive him everywhere with due honour as the king's knight' (*CPR*, 1258–66, p. 638).

[5] *Cal. Cl. R.* (1297), pp. 33–34. See Clowes, *History of the Royal Navy*, pp. 112 f., 208–9 (for Letters of Marque and Reprisals).

quoted *Fasciculus de Superioritate Maris* is ascribed to 1297.[1]

The families of Charles and Alard were equally at home in England and Gascony. Edward Charles was an English knight from Norfolk,[2] but Andrew Charles was named with the merchants of Bayonne who were attacked by Spanish sailors within the power of Portugal.[3] The Alards were a Winchelsea family. Gervase Alard, who commanded the Western Fleet, was buried in the church, where his skeleton was found wrapped in lead some years ago. Justin Alard was one of the Cinque Ports Captains in 1300 and Thomas Alard a bailiff of Winchelsea. The form of these names suggests a mercantile and possibly Gascon origin.

A more traditional type of admiral was Lord Simon de Montague, a king's banneret and a baron, appointed in 1307 as Captain and Governor of the whole fleet. Simon, who bore *golden griffins on a blue banner* at Caerlaverock,[4] was Constable of Corfe and later Beaumaris. He is said to have served in all Edward's wars.[5]

After 1293 the war, not yet declared on land, was growing in intensity between merchant fleets at sea, and the control of this in the interests of the king and his subjects led to the appointment, for the first time, of admirals. There was as yet no Royal Navy, though the king had a ship or two, and important men like the Earl of Aumale

---

[1] *Foed.*, p. 562. The *Fasciculus* is in the PRO, and was described in an account of an exhibition of Naval Records there in *The Times* newspaper dated 21 September 1950. There is a translation in Sir H. Nicolas, *History of the Royal Navy*, i. 308–13.

[2] PRA, no. 573 (Norfolk).

[3] *Cal. Cl. R.* (2 August 1294), p. 363, cf. pp. 353–4. Next year the men of Portsmouth intercepted and took 15 Spanish ships bound for Flanders (Rishanger, *Annales*, pp. 150–1). It was Robert Charles who in 1270 sold everything he had and took the Cross, whereupon the king moved to pity granted him 400 marks (*CPR*, p. 434).

[4] The *Song* (no. 65) simplifies his arms, which were *Quartile de argent e de azure. En les quarters de azure les greffons de or. En les quarters de argent les daunces de goulis* (PRA, 149).

[5] Simon de Montague castellated Yerdlingham, co. Somerset. He was appointed 30 January 1307 (*CPR*, p. 490).

before 1261, the Earl Marshal in the 'seventies, and John Botetourt are known to have had their own ships. The nucleus for a war-time fleet was provided, under a standing agreement, by the Cinque Ports, and the rest were, like their crews, impressed from other ports as need arose.[1] Like the army on land the crews had from time to time to be prosecuted because they 'withdrew without licence', as in 1302 and 1303, or otherwise defaulted.[2] The ships, merely armed merchantmen, with soldiers on board if battle was intended, sailed in convoy.[3] As on land, the opposing sides sometimes agreed upon a time and place for battle. This is said to have happened on 14 April 1293 when Sir Robert Tiptoft, a baron, Justiciar of South Wales (1281–6) and Constable of Nottingham Castle from 1275 till his death in 1297, led a fleet of sixty ships to the capture of the whole French fleet—240 vessels— under Charles of Valois.[4]

John Botetourt's long and active career began in or before 1285, when (as in 1286 and 1290) he is listed among the king's knights (bachelors). His origin is mysterious, for an entry in the Hailes Abbey Chronicle is said by Mr. H. G. Richardson[5] to show that he was an illegitimate son of Edward I. This is not reflected in his arms, for he bore *Or*, a saltire engrailed *Sable*.[6] How-

---

[1] *Cal. Cl. R.* (1297), p. 41. Order to impress all ships north of Trent of over 4 tuns' burthen.

[2] *CPR*, pp. 52–53, 61. Twenty towns were involved.

[3] *Cal. Cl. R.* (1301), pp. 499–501.

[4] Clowes, *History of the Royal Navy*, i. 205. For Tiptoft as Constable see *C. Fine Rolls*, vol. i, pp. 39, 56, 129, 401, 447, 508; vol. ii, pp. 2–3. Langtoft and Trivet put the action in May, not April. 'Tibetot' bears *Az.* a saltire engrailed *Gu.* as no. 196 on the Dering Roll. His son Payn is no. 54, PRA, and 141 Dunstable.

[5] Cott. MS., Cleop. D. iii, fol. 51, cited in *Handbook of British Chronology*, p. 35.

[6] Falkirk no. 74, *PRA*, no. 55. The Caerlaverock Roll (no. 46) appears to be in error in saying that he had *jaune banière ot e penon* (ed. T. Wright, p. 14). His gold banner would naturally be blazoned as yellow in the *Song*, but the pennon cannot be explained away. He had been a banneret for two years at the time of the siege (e.g. he is no. 74 on the Falkirk Roll, where his retinue included Robert de Felton (PRA, Gloucs., 882) and John de Poeveres (PRA,

ever, his first recorded appearance suggests that he could have been born about 1265; this would fit in with the date of his death—1324. Some support for this view may be found in the assertion of the Italian chronicler Villani, that Edward fell in love about Easter 1265, when he was a prisoner in Dover Castle, with a lady sent by his mother to help him escape.[1]

The Botetourts were an East Anglian family,[2] and John seals the letter to the Pope as Lord of Mendlesham in Suffolk.[2] He had command of the North Sea Fleet in 1294 and again in 1315.[3] This reappointment is surprising in that it seems to ignore his action in 1312 when he was Constable of Framlingham Castle, held for the king as a Bigod escheat. He was, according to a document[4] that has not been traced, 'Confederate with Guy de Beauchamp, Earl of Warwick in surprising of Piers de Gaveston at Deddington in co. Oxon. upon St. Barnabas' Eve, he published a special writing under his Hand and Seal in justification thereof, promising to live and die with the Earl in that quarrel'.[5]

Most of John Botetourt's campaigns were on land. One of them is of special interest, in spite of a total lack of information as to what happened, for the composition of the force under command. This is his foray, or perhaps only

Essex, 443) as his knights. His brother Guy and William Botetout his esquire (*valet*) were with him at Falkirk (Bain, p. 287). I think Guy was the eldest (*Cal. Cl. R.* 1290, p. 113).

[1] *Croniche*, vii. 39. But there is no hint of the lady's identity in the Montfort Household Roll of the period. Villani is writing fifty years after the event.

[2] Other members of the Botetourt family were associated with Norfolk: Guy (PRA, 541) occurs as early as 1267 (*Cl. R.*, p. 398) and 1276 (*Cal. Cl. R.*, p. 338); William (PRA, 542 = 205 Dunst., *de la commune*); Rauf (PRA, 543, a 'Swan' Knight); Thomas (PRA, 580 = 206 Dunst., *de la commune*), and Roger called 'Bottitourte', Bliss, *Cal. Pap. Lett.* i. 549.

[3] Bottetourt's commission as Admiral in 1315 is given in full in Clowes, *History of the Navy*, i. 142–3.

[4] Dugdale, *Baronage*, ii. 46. 'Ex autog. penes T. Co. Elgin'.

[5] At the time of his death he held a third of the barony of Beauchamp of Bedford jointly with his wife Maud, whom he married 30 Ed. I, *Cal. IPM*, vol. vi, no. 587 (*c*. 30 Nov. 1324). He was summoned to Parliament as a baron 1–18 Ed. II.

an intended foray, into Scotland on 9 January 1304, as Captain and Justiciar of Galloway, Annan, and the valley of Nith. Botetourt led three bannerets, with sixteen, thirteen, and nine squires respectively; sixteen knights with six squires; forty-two valets and nineteen hobelars. The valets I take to be of the same military status as the squires but not personally attached to a knight. This however is probably not capable of proof for this occasion. There were also 2,736 foot with their captains and corporals from Cumberland, Westmorland, and Lancashire.[1]

The navy was not so well paid as the army. Sailors received 3*d.* a day, masters 6*d.*, and an Admiral of the Fleet 2*s.*—a bachelor's pay.[2]

[1] Bain, *Cal. Docs. Scot.* ii, no. 377.
[2] See Liber *Quotidianus . . . Garderobe*, pp. 271 ff.

III

THE EARLY ROLLS AND THE HERALDS

(1) GLOVER'S ROLL

THE first of the extant rolls, Glover's Roll, now exists only in sixteenth-century transcripts. There are three versions, whose textual history is as complicated as that of any classical manuscript or medieval romance.[1] An original belonged to 'Mr. Harvey of Leicester' in or before 1586. It seems possible that the roll was acquired by 'Mr. Harvey' about the time of the famous revels at Kenilworth in 1575, when Robert Dudley, Earl of Leicester, entertained Queen Elizabeth with Masques and Revelry. It is likely that Mr. Harvey belonged to a new family, the Harveys of Saffron Walden. Of six brothers Gabriel, the eldest, is well known and the Earl of Leicester was his patron. Another brother Richard (1560–1623?), the enemy of Thomas Nash in *Strange News* (1592),[2] had antiquarian interests and was also patronized by Leicester. He wrote *Philadelphus or a Defense of Brutus and the Brutans History* and dedicated it to the earl, and it is he who may be concealed beneath the style 'Mr. Harvey of Leicester'.[3]

Harvey's version contains 217 coats of which the last six are early-fourteenth-century additions: too many for a

---

[1] *CEMRA*, pp. 3–9.

[2] *Shakespeare's England*, p. 231.

[3] See the *DNB* for this family. There is clearly no question of William Harvey, Clarenceux (*fl.* 1567), or the great William Harvey, M.D. (1578–1657), the medical pioneer, though the latter could be implicated in point of time and opportunity.

baronage, too few for a knightage.[1] It begins with the king, his son, and all the earls, but then becomes highly selective. It is closely connected with the court and household of Henry III. There are nine stewards of the household, a butler, chamberlains, members of the Lord Edward's household,[2] at least four of Simon de Montfort's fellow crusaders,[3] as well as Poitevins[4] and Bretons.[5] This reflects the state of Henry III's court before the baronage and officials had split into opposing factions. The struggle for power was still purely domestic and the aliens were still firmly in the saddle.

About 1255 is suggested as the date, a period of some heraldic activity, for the Lord Edward was knighted on 13 October 1254, was initiated into the use of arms at the tournament at Blyth in June 1256,[6] and saw his first active service in Gwynedd in August.

But this is not an occasional roll, and the original painted roll must have been begun before 1252 because Nicholas de Sandford, who died in 1252, here occurs with his father and bears a blue label on his arms. But before he died, as Matthew Paris shows, he had dropped the label.[7] So Harvey's version represents the heraldic situation in or prior to 1252, with later additions, and this is in line with the supposed date of Grimaldi's version.[8]

Now Simon de Montfort occupies a unique position on this roll. He had returned from Gascony to England towards Christmas 1251 and left again for Gascony on 16 June

[1] Harvey's version was edited by Nicholas Harris Nicolas (William Pickering, 1829) as 'A Roll of Arms compiled in the reign of Henry III, MCCXLV', *CEMRA*, p. 5.

[2] Ebulo de Montibus (no. 103), Nicholas de Molis (or Meules) seneschal of Gascony 1244 and one of the king's marshals under de Montfort in 1248 (*Cl.R.*, p. 119), and Edward's *nutriator* in 1243 (no. 82); Dru de Barentin (no. 83) and Stephen Longespée, seneschal of Gascony, 1255–7, and sometime Justiciar of Ireland (no. 182).

[3] Thomas and William Furnivall, Hugh Wake, and Amaury de St. Amand.

[4] Guy de Rocheford (no. 203).   [5] Robert de Morteyn.

[6] See my 'Tournament in the Thirteenth Century', p. 256.

[7] *Chron. Maj.* v, p. 273. Glover's Roll nos. 110, 111.

[8] *CEMRA*, p. 7.

1252, after defending his conduct as seneschal against the king and other accusers. It is to this period that the earliest version of the roll is tentatively assigned. It looks like Leicester's roll, and I think Mr. Harvey of Leicestershire obtained it from the neighbouring castle of Kenilworth, perhaps during the revels.

Simon de Montfort, Earl of Leicester and Steward of England, seems to have regarded himself—if the roll is a trustworthy witness—as having precedence over everyone except the king's brother, Richard, Earl of Cornwall. Not only does his name precede that of the Marshal, but he boasts two armorial devices: his personal shield of arms, and his banner as Steward of England. This could be taken as an indication of his consciousness that the Stewardship might be politically useful to him.

Admitted as earl in 1230, Simon had officiated as *Senescallus Anglie* at Henry III's wedding in 1236,[1] and had aroused great opposition by his clandestine marriage with the king's sister in 1238, but his high-handed behaviour as Seneschal of Gascony had resulted in a violent personal quarrel with Henry at Westminster, after which the earl returned to Gascony, and until April 1258 his relations with the crown were amicable.[2] The stages by which he emerged as leader of the rebellion against the king are notoriously obscure. It is accepted that he was 'one of the six barons who formed the sworn confederacy of 12 April 1258 which was the germ of the revolution'.[3] He was also one of the twenty-four framers of the Provisions of Oxford, one of the Council of Fifteen, and of the twenty-four to negotiate an aid. But 'the Earl Marshal,

[1] Matt. Par., *Chron. Maj.* iii. 336–9.
[2] Simon was employed on embassies to Scotland in August 1254 and to France, with Peter of Savoy, in January 1256. He also received 'other marks of confidence and distinction' (Ramsay, op. cit., p. 167, citing *Foed.* i. 306, *Royal Letters*, ii, 107, 120, 121, 392, 393).
[3] R. F. Treharne, 'The Role of Simon de Montfort, 1258–65', being the Raleigh Lecture to the British Academy (1954) published in their *Proceedings*, vol. xl, pp. 75–102. See pp. 81–82 of that work.

Roger Bigod, was spokesman of the barons, and received and kept the sealed copy of the King's Oath to observe the Provisions'.[1] During another lull in 1260, at the knighting of the king's new son-in-law John of Brittany, Simon allowed Henry of Almaine to perform the office of Steward as his deputy.[1] In return the Lord Edward opened the ceremonies by knighting his two cousins, Leicester's sons, Henry and Simon.

Whether Simon de Montfort's undisputed claims to the Stewardship gave him any right to interfere in the management of the king's household or the government of the country was a matter which had not been openly raised. Simon himself in May 1265 appealed to his great-aunt, the ancient Loretta, Countess of Leicester, who had long been a recluse at Hackington near Canterbury, for information about the rights and liberties that appertained to the Stewardship of England in regard to the earldom and honour of Leicester.[2] About this time his style as *Senescallus Anglie* appears on the Close Rolls.[3] He was trying, in the few months that remained to him, to legalize his position. This emphatic claim of precedence for the Steward seems to be suggested in Glover's Roll, and if so appeared for the first time about 1251/2.

The coats assigned to Simon de Montfort and the Earldom of Leicester in Glover's Roll, the Heralds' Roll, and the PRA help to illuminate the varied history of the office of Steward of England in this period. On Glover's Roll, as on the PRA, the arms of the Earldom of Leicester are given as *Gules a lion rampant Argent with a forked tail.* Glover's Roll also gives the charge on Simon's banner as Steward as *party per pale Argent and Gules.* The Heralds' Roll confuses the issue by assigning this charge on the

---

[1] *Foed.* i. 402.

[2] *Close Rolls* (1263–5), pp. 115–16. See Vernon Harcourt, *His Grace the Steward,* pp. 125–6, for a translation, and F. M. Powicke, 'Loretta, Countess of Leicester', in *Historical Essays in Honour of James Tait* (Manchester, 1933), and C. Bémont, *Simon de Montfort,* ed. E. F. Jacob, pp. 9–15.

[3] *Close Rolls* (20 March 1265), p. 37. Cf. *CPR*, p. 416.

banner to the Earl of Leicester (no. 50) and giving the
lion coat to 'Earl Symound' (no. 47), as if they were two
distinct persons, or as if there had been an Earl of Leicester
who had used the banner charge without the lion. There
was indeed room for confusion in the history of the
Stewardship, for Edmund Crouchback was created Earl of
Leicester and Steward of England by a document dated
25 October 1265. But this deed was never sealed: it remained an 'escrow', and on the same day Edmund was
granted the Earldom without the Stewardship. We hear
next that in November 1268, at the Parliament of
Winchester, the Lord Edward was made Steward and
was granted all the castles in England.[1] Finally in May
1269 the Stewardship was granted to Edmund for life,
after Edward had held it for six months.[2] So in theory the
office was in abeyance from the death of Simon de Montfort till 1269, with the exception of Edward's brief tenure
of it, for which Winchester annals are the only authority.
This was perhaps done to emphasize the complete authority
of the Crown, and to give an official cloak to the reality
of power exercised by the Lord Edward at this time.

(II) THE HERALDS' ROLL

The existing Heralds' Roll is only a mutilated fragment,
chopped up and pasted into a book in the seventeenth
century, of a thirteenth-century painted roll. This original
was conflated with much extraneous material to form, in
the Fitzwilliam version, a roll of seventeen membranes containing some 697 shields painted in colour. The Fitzwilliam version[3] is a fifteenth-century copy of (?) an early

---

[1] *Ann. Wint.* (RS), p. 107. See my *Richard of Cornwall*, p. 145, for the context
of these events.

[2] The fact that it was only for life was repeated in grants of 1274 and 1275
(*Foed.*, p. 515, August 1274, from Liber 'A' and *Cal. Cl. R.*, p. 81 (27 February
1275)).

[3] MS. 297 in the Fitzwilliam Museum in Cambridge. See for this and the
other versions *A.W.*, pp. 9–14. The Heralds' Roll, once called Planché's Roll,

fourteenth-century roll. The Heralds' Roll itself appears to have been a compact and well-ordered document, but the 'versions' do not seem to have been inspired by any principle other than that of mere agglomeration. As in the Camden Roll, with which I believe it to be contemporary, the earls do not form a group at the beginning, but are scattered throughout the roll.[1]

With this roll we pass for a moment into a realm of pure fantasy, in which the heroes of romance are assigned coats of arms side by side with actual Edwardian knights. The Heralds' Roll is indeed unique in containing ladies—though they frequented tournaments throughout the century—foreign princes, and legendary heroes all together. It marks the culminating point of the Arthurian cult in England. It marks too the point when European interests, rather than those of Wales or Scotland, are of paramount importance. A third feature is the appearance of the colourful and anomalous Anthony Bek, Bishop of Durham and Patriarch of Jerusalem, the only ecclesiastic found upon any of the Rolls mentioned in this book.

Wykes[2] tells us that 120 knights, of whom 22 were bannerets, took the Cross at Northampton in 1268, and there are on the Patent rolls long lists of protections for four years from 1270 for those (including Queen Eleanor) who had taken the Cross. Edward himself had protection for five years.[3] But this is not to say that all went, or that all who went reached Palestine. Edmund of Cornwall

---

is printed in *The Genealogist* (N.S.), iii (1886), 148–55, 240–4; iv. 17–22, 197–203; v. 173–9.

[1] The deceased earls include Winchester (1244), Aumale (1260), and de Insula (1262). The Rey de Gfunye of the Heralds' version is the Rey de Gryfonie on the Fitzwilliam version (no. 16) and, with colours reversed, no. 17 on Camden's Roll. The Rey de — who is no. 18 on the Fitzwilliam version is the Rey de Bealme, bearing *Az.* 3 barges in pale *Arg.* on Camden's Roll no. 12. No. 169 Fitzwilliam (*Or*, a bear passant *Sa.* muzzled *Arg.* for Reginald FitzUrs) is perhaps intended to be for one of the murderers (or a descendant) of Thomas Becket. 'Bealme' is perhaps Bethlehem, for Jerusalem.

[2] *Chron. T. Wykes* (RS), p. 218.

[3] *CPR*, pp. 411, 424, 425, 439, 479–80, 588.

returned on the murder of Henry of Almain at Viterbo in 1270. Thomas de Clare came home in 1272. Robert Charles sold everything that he had in order to go, and Edward was so moved by pity that he gave him 400 marks.[1] Payn de Chaworth and Robert Tibetot received in 1273 600 marks from the Legate for going, Roger Lyburn had 1,000 marks from the Legate for going, but he kept the money and stayed at home. In 1272 he was ordered by the Pope to refund it.[2] St. Louis had pressed Gilbert de Clare, Earl of Gloucester, to accompany Edward and he is said to have crossed to France with 100 knights on 24 February 1270,[3] but if so, he soon returned without going further.[4] The only earl to accompany Edward was Edmund of Lancaster.

The romantic side of chivalry—courtly love and minstrelsy—is essentially bound up with the position of women in medieval society; the cult of the Blessed Virgin Mary and its rapid spread in the thirteenth century went hand in hand with the blossoming of the Arthurian legend. Ladies were passionately interested, or pretended to be, in tournaments and romances. Can we assume that great ladies were interested in the coats of arms of their husbands' friends? There is a gate to Caernarvon called the Queen's Gate: there are Eleanor Crosses all over the country. I do not think it too fanciful to suggest that this is the Eleanor Roll of Arms, including the Arthurian heroes whom she encouraged her husband to emulate. Her parents are also on the Roll. The making of such a roll is consonant with what is known of, or what was believed to be true of, the tastes and character of Eleanor of Castile: 'Erat enim quasi columna totius Anglie, sexu quidem foemina, sed animo atque virtute plus viro.'[5]

---

[1] Ibid., p. 434.   [2] Cal. Pap. Lett., pp. 444–5.
[3] Gerv. Cant., p. 248.
[4] Gloucester was ordered to stop fortifying Portland in Dorset on 14 September 1270 (Close Rolls, p. 292).
[5] Trokelowe (RS), pp. 49–50, written after 1307, continues that in Eleanor's lifetime the aliens in England were not harshly treated, and Rishanger (p. 121)

We have on the Heralds' Roll the whole apparatus of medieval chivalry and romance: it forms a perfect backcloth for the Swan Knight, the Feast of the Swans, and the opening on 19 April 1278 of the tomb of King Arthur at Glastonbury by Edward and his Queen.[1] The coat of arms of the King of Armenia reminds us that his envoys were received on 28 May 1277 and Tartar envoys at Easter.[2] The King of Scotland with a small entourage was present at the marriage of Llewelyn to Eleanor de Montfort at Worcester on 13 October 1278, and Scottish homage was done, to Edward's great joy. Finally on 23 May 1279 the king and queen were in Paris, and homage was done for the newly acquired counties of Ponthieu and Aumale, both on the roll, on the occasion of the Treaty of Amiens with France. This roll, with its manifold interests and sympathies, symbolizes Edward at the height of his real power, ruling over a country that was richer and more powerful than ever before.

Edward's prolonged tour of Europe (1270–4) and sojourn at Acre (1271–2) while on Crusade, no less than the Treaty of Amiens in 1279, account for the many foreign coats on a roll of this date. There is no list extant of those who accompanied Edward to the Holy Land, where he is said to have had about a thousand knights. The English sources, especially the chronicles of Hemingburgh and Wykes, do not report any serious fighting during Edward's stay in Palestine, which he left in August 1272. The illness of the old king Henry III at Westminster, culminating in his death in November 1272 while Edward was still abroad, together with the murder

says that she was *Anglicorum amatrix omnium.* Eleanor of Castile was much involved with the Jews, whereas the Queen Mother, Eleanor of Provence who outlived her, hated them. There is some account of Eleanor of Castile's household in Tout, chap. v, 236 ff., and a mention of the *querele* against her 'ministers' on her death, ibid., p. 271.

[1] T. D. Kendrick, *British Antiquity* (1950), p. 98, gives a picture of the lead cross found in Arthur's tomb. Leland saw and described it.

[2] *CPR*, p. 265.

of Henry of Almaine, his nephew, in 1270 and the death of Edward's son and heir John on 1 August of that year, must have done much to mar any pleasure that Edward derived from an expedition so devoid of military interest. That Edward was a fine horseman and a fine lance we gather from other evidence, and he certainly legislated for the favourite sport of his youth in the *Statutum Armorum*.[1] But nothing is added to our knowledge of his chivalrous prowess by any information from Palestine. Moreover, apart from the jousting tour of 1260 in France and the rough and tumble of the 'Little Battle' of Chalon on the way home from the Holy Land, nothing is known of Edward's participation in joust or tourney. It is a matter for surprise and regret that no roll survives to celebrate his fame in either. The Heralds' Roll is the one that comes nearest to providing a heraldic commentary on his chivalrous career and the Arthurian interests of the age.[2]

The Heralds' Roll brings us closer than any other to the Arthurian interests of Edward I and his court, and is convincing testimony to the lasting influence of the Arthurian cult in the chivalrous society of the age. It culminated in the Feast of the Swans in 1306, when Edward I, before setting out on his last campaign to conquer Scotland, held a great mass-investiture at Westminster, where more than 250 young men were knighted, followed by a banquet in the Palace known to modern writers as the Feast of the Swans, since two swans formed the main dish, and upon these birds chivalrous vows were sworn by the guests in honour of the occasion.[3]

[1] See 'The Tournament in England', in *Essays presented to F. M. Powicke* (Oxford, 1948). In 1286 Edward had his armour enlarged, at the age of 47 (PRO, E. 101/351/28), when he was celebrating the conquest of Wales.

[2] It may be that the Church preferred to ignore the Arthurian cult. Archbishop Pecham, in defending clerical liberties against the king, summarized the history of England from Roman times. But he jumps from Constantine to Wihtred, knowing nothing of Arthur or the Brut (*Registrum* (RS), i. 242–3).

[3] See 'The Song of Caerlaverock and the Parliamentary Roll of Arms', by the present writer, in *Proc. of the British Academy* for 1962.

The symbolism of the Swans which here found expression is an obscure but recurrent thread in thirteenth-century epic literature, and is perhaps best known as part of the Lohengrin story. It is particularly associated in England with the Thony (or Tony) family. Matthew Paris remarks that Roger de Tony was descended from those famous knights *qui a Cignis nomine intitulantur* and promises, in vain, to expand this obscure remark.[1] The herald-minstrel who wrote the *Song of Caerlaverock* thus blazons Robert de Tony's shield:

> Escu blanc, e baniere blanche
> O la vermeille manche

and remarks that he well shows that he is descended from the Counts of Boulogne, who also claimed this fabulous descent.[2]

Robert de Thony or Tony of Painscastle or Castle Maud near Radnor, the Swan Knight of the *Song of Caerlaverock*, was a baron of the southern Welsh march, as his nephew Fulk FitzWarin of Whittington in Shropshire—another hero of fact and fiction—was of the northern.[3] Two earlier members of the family are described by Matthew Paris as cousins of the King of Scots. These were Richard, who had been Treasurer of Anjou, and Ralph, both of whom died in 1252.[4] Thony served in Flanders in 1297 with two knights and twelve esquires, and was promoted banneret on 1 November 1297.[5] At Falkirk next year he led a similar troop of two knights and twelve valets or esquires.[6] In 1301 he was of the Prince's

---

[1] R. Vaughan, *Matthew Paris* (Cambridge, 1958), pp. 89, 177, citing the *Gesta Abbatum*.

[2] *Song of Caerlaverock*, no. 68. Cf. PRA 49, which entry has been marked with daggers for deletion to indicate that Tony had died since the Roll was made. The name occurs again in the supplementary list of *abatues*, as PRA 1049.

[3] H. Johnstone, *Edward of Caernarvon*, p. 74.

[4] Matt. Par., *Chron. Maj.* v, p. 298.   [5] N. B. Lewis, loc. cit.

[6] H. Gough, *Scotland in 1298* (1888), p. 37. After Falkirk Thony was owed £118. 16s. 8d. by the Crown for 'restor de chevaux e pur ses gages qi ariere li soit ausint' (ibid., pp. 257–8, from Privy Seal writs of 18, 20 October, 26 Ed. I).

bodyguard in Scotland.[1] Both Thony and others deserted in 1306.[2] His last appearance is as head of the group called *De la Commune* at the Dunstable tournament in 1309. He died in September 1309.[3]

A great number of the persons mentioned on this roll might have been met by the crusaders in the course of their journey, e.g. the Doge of Venice.[4] But this is not a record of casual encounters; the roll is not in any sense occasional, even if the word be stretched to cover the whole epoch of the Crusade. For example, at Bologna Edward lodged with the Count of Lanzavecchia, but he is not commemorated on the roll.[5] Yet such an excursion offered great heraldic opportunities, and it is known that English minstrels went with the royal party. There was also Mr. Richard, a clerk of Queen Eleanor, who made and illuminated for her at Acre in 1271 a copy of Vegetius' *De Re Militari*, perhaps intended as a present from the Queen to her husband. This manual on the art of war was highly esteemed in the thirteenth century. It had helped, according to Salimbene, to inspire the defence of Milan against the Emperor Frederick II during the famous siege.[6]

[1] Johnstone, op. cit., p. 77.   [2] Dugdale, *Bar.* i. 471.

[3] *Cal. IPM*, vol. v, no. 198. Tony was a tenant and sometime follower of the Earl of Hereford.

[4] The Fitzwilliam or long version of the roll includes about 400 English and 264 foreign counts and knights. There is a full complement of 20 English and 5 Scottish earls, but no Welshmen.

[5] The count, one of the Lanzavecchias of Alessandria, was at that time *Capitano del popolo* at Bologna. Edward promised to knight him when he came to England, and they later exchanged letters on this subject (*Foed.* 523, dated 18 May 1275 from Milan, and Edward's reply dated 15 October 1275, ibid. 529).

[6] *Scriptorium*, tom. vi, no. i, pp. 39–50, 'Maistre Richard, a thirteenth century translator of the *De Re Militari* of Vegetius [Renatus, a fourth-century writer]', by Lewis Thorpe. This work has been translated into English by John Clark, under the title 'Flavius Vegetius Renatus, *Military Institutions of the Romans* (Harrisburg, Penn., 1944). The manuscript made in 1271 is now in the Fitzwilliam Museum at Cambridge, among the Add. MSS. of the Marley collection. The illumination shows Vegetius as bearded, but Edward and his six knights are tall and clean-shaven. (For a twelfth-century parallel see A. L. Poole, *From Domesday Book to Magna Carta* (1951), p. 373.)

It was on Crusade, too, that Edward asked Rusticieno da Pisa to translate his

The really remarkable feature of the Heralds' Roll, and one that makes it unique, is the presence of ladies upon it. Yet it should not, in view of the presence of ladies at tournaments and their fondness for romances, be thought surprising. It is in keeping with the whole conception of medieval chivalry that Edward's wife, Eleanor of Castile, and his mother, Eleanor of Provence, should be included, though the latter did not go on Crusade. The roll reflects the atmosphere of the time and the foreign experience of the Heralds who were in the royal party. Eleanor of Castile is one of the few ladies known to have ventured on Crusade with or without her husband. The feminine interest of the roll may explain the strong romantic element—the inclusion of Prester John (but only in the long version), and Sir Bevis of Hampton who fought against the Danes; or of Roland, the Crusader against the Moors, and Sir Gawayn, celebrated in the contemporary romance of Sir Gawayn and the Green Knight.

The story of the attempt on Edward's life when he was at Acre cannot be controlled in detail though it is alluded to years later in papal letters.[1] This took place on 17 June 1271 when an emissary of the Old Man of the Mountain, against whose Assassins Richard of Cornwall had already warned Henry III,[2] tried to stab Edward. When the royal attendants came running at the noise of the scuffle, they found that Edward had already killed his assailant, whereupon his Minstrel seized a stool and dashed out the man's brains with it. According to an embroidered version Eleanor sucked the poison from the wound.[3] Eleanor, too, carried

prose collection of Arthurian romances into French from the royal copy. This Rusticianus was the man who wrote down in French the travels of Marco Polo, when they were fellow prisoners in 1298. See Mr. Cedric E. Pickford's apt summary of Edward's Arthurian interests in *Yorkshire Archaeological Journal*, xxxviii (1954), 'The Three Crowns of King Arthur', pp. 373–82, and R. S. Loomis, 'Edward I, Arthurian Enthusiast', in *Speculum* (1953), xxviii. 114–27.

[1] Bain, *Cal. Docs. Scot.*, no. 469, and Bliss, *Cal. Pap. Lett.*, no. 467.
[2] *Ann. Burton*, pp. 392–5.
[3] Hemingburgh (old ed.), pp. 334–7. Cf. *Fl. Wig. Cont.*, p. 210; Wykes, p. 250; *Lib. de Ant. Leg.*, p. 156; *Flores Hist.* iii. 23–24.

the bones of Guinevere, we are told, while Edward carried the bones of Arthur at the ceremonial opening of Arthur's tomb at Glastonbury in 1279.[1]

Part of the interest of the story of the Assassin is that it is one of the two occasions on which Edward is reported to have spoken in English, the other being 'that simple and irreverent pun upon Bigod'.[2] But no one has shown that Edward could *read* English, or indeed anything else.[3] Though the bulk of the population was English, and theirs the language of the shire and hundred courts, the king and his courtiers spoke French (or rather Anglo-Norman). But the continuity of spoken English was ensured by the emergence of the country gentry as an articulate class in touch not only with their tenants but with Westminster. English survived in the sermon, in devotional literature,[4] and in the local courts of law, and so the way was kept open for the efflorescence of the fourteenth century with Chaucer and Langland. But when Edward I was a child the prestige of French culture was at its height. Edward's mother-tongue was Provençal, a language more akin to Spanish than to northern French, but for king and nobles and cloistered ladies French was the language of everyday life, of conciliar memoranda, privy seal writs, the language of their business letters and private correspondence. Their leisure hours were amused by French romances and poems—but in thirteenth-century England even French had to be taught in local schools.[5]

---

[1] Ad. of Domerham, p. 588.

[2] Coulton, *Medieval Panorama*, p. 227, cites this as the only known occasion upon which Edward spoke English. Professor Tout, *Edward I*, p. 6, was more optimistic: 'French, Latin, and English he could understand with equal facility.' It is Hemingburgh who says, in the Assassin story, *Et ait Edwardus in Anglico*.

[3] Professor V. H. Galbraith allows himself the guarded remark that Edward was 'highly educated' in his Raleigh Lecture on 'The Literacy of Mediaeval English Kings' (British Academy, 10 July 1935), but in his valuable paper on 'Nationality and Language' in *T.R. Hist. Soc.*, 4th ser., xxiii (1941), 113–28, the same writer does not bring the question under notice.

[4] e.g. the *Ancrene Riwle* and the *Ormulum*. See further R. W. Chambers, *The Continuity of English Prose*, pp. lxxxviii–xc.

[5] Trevisa complains of the decay in the teaching of French in schools, where it

In the romance 'Blonde of Oxford' the young French hero, Johan of Dammartin, made love to the Earl of Oxford's daughter by teaching her better French. In the same story the Earl of Gloucester speaks bad French.[1]

Latin was quite another matter. Edward's aunt Margaret always wrote to her brother Henry III in Latin, but unless upon a matter so formal that the king probably would not personally see the letter, she always wrote to her nephew in French.[2] This in itself raises a slight presumption that Edward preferred French to Latin. The matter seems to be clinched by a letter in which the dowager Duchess of Brunswick in 1280 complained of the behaviour of her brother, Henry of Granson, bishop-postulate of Verdun, whom Edward knew very well. The letter was in Latin, and the bearer was a chaplain who did not know French, so the Duchess asked Edward to provide him with a clerk who knew Latin *ut illo mediante, vos de negotio nostro . . . valeat expedire*.[3] The duchess assumes that the letter, like all medieval correspondence, would be read aloud by the bearer, and translated by the clerk from Latin into French. If Edward had known enough Latin to understand a formal letter this procedure would have been unnecessary.

(III) HERALDS, MINSTRELS, AND ESCHEATORS

(*a*) Heralds and Minstrels

Throughout the time of Edward I and well on into the fourteenth century the minstrels and heralds are lumped together by the household clerks of the king under the marginal heading *Menestralli*. They had two kings, called *Rex Haraldorum* and *Alter Rex Haraldorum*.[4] We are left in

was being replaced by English, so that scholars knew no more French 'than my left heele' (*Polychronicon* (RS), ii. 160, 161).
[1] There is a useful summary of this romance in E. Lavisse, *Histoire de France* (Paris, 1901), III. ii. pp. 362–6.
[2] Champollion-Figeac, *Lettres des Rois*, tome I, *passim*.
[3] *Foed.* I, ii, 588, 'ex autog.'   [4] See further Appendix A.

no doubt that everything pertaining to heraldry or minstrelsy came under their charge. A possible theory is that
the one king was more especially in charge of the minstrelsy proper and the other of their armorial functions.
The two careers were even at that time not clearly distinguished, and there were still king's minstrels who were
not heralds.[1] The *Song of Caerlaverock* (A.D. 1300) affords
abundant proof that a herald, probably one in the retinue
of a magnate, could still be a minstrel.[2]

Of the magnates, only those who regularly undertook
diplomatic negotiations with foreign powers stood in
need of heralds, who are thus found associated with the
Marches of Scotland, Wales, and Dover. There should
have been one at Durham—Bek was not the man to do
without one—and one, like Chandos Herald, who wrote
the life of the Black Prince, for Gascony (cf. Simon de
Montfort's so-called *barbitonsor*). If not Kings of Arms
they would be styled Harpers or Minstrels, of whom there
were a great number, as is attested by the list of those
present at the Feast of the Swans in 1306. In the list of
these the heralds, even the kings, are still named with the
minstrels. The list[3] begins thus:

Solutio facta diversis Menestrallis

Le Roy de Champaigne ⎫	
Le Roy Capenny ⎪	
Le Roy Baisescue ⎬ 5 marks each	
Le Roy Marchis ⎪	
Le Roy Robert ⎭	
Philippe de Caumbereye	60s.

---

[1] E. K. Chambers, in his classic work on *The Medieval Stage,* seems unaware
that his Minstrel Kings were more than strolling players. He has nothing to say
of the rise in status of some of them with the growth of heraldry. But the identity
of names leaves no room for doubt that the Minstrel Kings were Kings of Arms.

[2] Richard of Cornwall, as a boy in 1215, was accompanied by two trumpeters who would be classed as minstrels (*R. lit. pat.* ii. 197).

[3] E. K. Chambers, *The Medieval Stage,* App. C, p. 234, from Botfield,
Manners and Household Expenses (Roxburghe Club, 1840), from a Wardrobe
account.

The lesser minstrels follow, of whom one more king— le Roy Druet—receives 40s. The rest of the list includes Tabourers, Harpours, Gigours, Cithariste, le Waffror le Roy (one mark), Organists, Trumpeters, Crouderes, John Waffrarius Comitis Lancastrie (40d.).

Now this Roy Capenny or Caupenny also appears in 1290 at the wedding of Joan, daughter of Edward I, as King Caupenny of Scotland,[1] and in 1300 in John Droxford's Wardrobe account in the entry *Capigno Regi Haraldorum*, as the recipient of the price, as a gift, of a barded horse.[2] Possibly King Caupenny from Scotland is to be regarded as the predecessor of Lyon King of Arms. The Roy Robert of 1306 could be Robert Parvus (or le Petit?), King of the Heralds, who was paid at the rate of £2 a year as one of the two royal 'Kings of the Heralds' in 1290. The household account in which he occurs is important.[3] It has the heading *Menestralli* written vertically in the margin, opposite the following names:

John Drak Waffr[arius] Regis; Robert Parvus, Rex Haraldorum, 40s. each. John de Wyndesore, John de Barking, Adam Skyrewhit Escubis' Regis, 2 marks each. Nicholas Morel 'alteri Regi Haraldorum' 40s., Ricardinus vidulator (for the winter term only) 20s. John le Leutor (summer term only) 20s. Two 'trumpatores Regis' 40s. each.

The 'escubis' or possible 'escubif' I cannot interpret. The word might suggest cleaning, painting, or merely being in charge of shields. There had to be a Herald painter and this may be he. The list may point to a division into two Provinces (Norroy and Surroy) and also to the origin of two departments in the royal household, one of which went 'out of court' as the Heralds' College or the

---

[1] Chambers, op. cit., App. D, p. 238, citing 'Chappell li 15' = Botfield, op. cit., p. lxix, from a Wardrobe book of 18 Ed. I. PRA 1056 (*abatues*) gives Renaud de Coupenne *de goules a vj pennes de argent*. Cf. Arnold de Cava Penna, king's knight 1299–1300. Coupen is near Morpeth in Northumberland.

[2] PRO, E. 101/369/11, fol. 103ᵛ (Droxford's Wardrobe book).

[3] E. 101/352/24 (Household account 18–19 Ed. I).

College of Arms, the other (Nicholas Morel) being more akin to the Master of the King's Music.

From their treatment in the accounts of this period it appears that herald kings have a status similar to that of a poet laureate, like Henry of Avranches, in Henry III's reign. They are paid much less for their liveries than the knights, but in neither case does this payment bear much relation to their earning power. It is evident from the financial records of the Feast of the Swans that in 1306 there were still far more minstrels than heralds. This is so, too, at the marriage of Queen Eleanor of Castile's fifth daughter Margaret to John son of the Duke of Brabant in July 1290, when Walter de Storton, the king's harper, distributed £100, the gift of the bridegroom, among 426 minstrels, including Baston (sic) Noblet, the dancer of Liège.[1] All the great men of the time had their harpers (i.e. minstrels). At Falkirk in 1298 we find John le Harpur with Norfolk, Nicholas le Harpour with Oxford, John le Harpur with William de Cantilupe, John le Harper with Lancaster, and Richard le Harpour with Walter de Beauchamp, the Steward of the Royal Household.[2] But Percy is the only one with the King of Arms in his retinue. The rest are 'Minstrels' but not 'Kings'. It may be that persons who did not have ambassadorial or similar status *vis-à-vis* a foreign power would not need herald kings, but only 'minstrels' with heraldic knowledge. Hence the difference between the *Song of Caerlaverock* by (?) Clifford's minstrel and the Falkirk Roll of Arms by (?) Walter le Rey Marchis, but this is only a conjecture.

It is safe, then, to say that the more successful Edwardian minstrels had a knowledge of heraldry and could become Kings of Arms, for on some lists the same people are Kings of Minstrels who elsewhere are Kings of Heralds.

Hemingburgh, writing sixty years after the event, had

---

[1] Wardrobe book of 18 Ed. I cited by Botfield, p. lxix.
[2] H. Gough, *Scotland in 1298*, pp. 33, 39, 178, 181, 184.

a good source for the battle of Evesham, giving the names of the *vexilliferi* or bannerets killed, and containing the story of Margoth, Simon de Montfort's female spy, who went about dressed as a man. He also mentions *Nicholas barbitonsor qui expertus erat in cognicione armorum*, as the man who recognized the insignia of the royalist forces for Simon on the field of Evesham before the battle.[1] As a former Seneschal of Gascony and royal ambassador it sounds odd that Simon should have had to depend upon his barber for essential military information. It is not to be doubted that he *had* a barber,[2] and the uncertainty of a minstrel's employment may have led to this unusual doubling of parts.[3] From the thirteenth century until the nineteenth the Waffrers or Confectioners, too, are in the same company, partly because they are paid out of the Privy Purse. Chaucer in *The Pardoner's Tale* (l. 151) mentions 'Syngers with harpes, Baudes, Waferers', and Langland in *Piers Plowman* has 'Mynstrelcie can Ich nat muche, bote make men murye, as a waffrer with waffres'.[4] This evidence is displayed to remove any suspicion that the textual propinquity of the Waffrer and the Heralds might arouse as to any armorial significance in the Teutonic-sounding Waffrer.

The King of Arms has by the end of Edward I's reign long been established as a specialist in heraldry, who, under the Marshal, prohibited or proclaimed and officiated at tournaments, assisted the Marshal at Coronations, acted as ambassadors, or King's messengers, assisted at the creation of new knights, but probably did not

---

[1] Hemingburgh (Camden Soc., 1957), pp. 200 f. (= old ed. i. 322–5).

[2] The Lord Edward had one in the same year (Botfield, *Manners and Household Expenses*, p. 9, payment of 6*d.* to the Lord Edward's *barbitonsor*).

[3] Geoffrey de Lusignan is said to have had an 'Ystrio' (? minstrel) called Elyas le Barber who on 18 December 1256 received a suitable robe of the King's gift (*Cl. R.* (1256), p. 17). A possible rationalization of the *barbitonsor* is that the story, circulating in a vernacular script, referred to a Harpour or Harper in which the *h* was read as *b* and the long *p* as *b*.

[4] C. xvi. 199. The Wafery was still a Privy Purse department in 1830. See *OED* s.v. *Waffrer*, whence I take these two quotations.

themselves entertain the king with song and dance as did the lesser minstrels listed with them in the records.

On one corner of this dark subject, already illuminated by Sir Anthony Wagner, a little further light may now be thrown. Walter le Rey Marchis or Walter le Marchis seems to have started his career in the retinue of Sir Henry Percy, Warden of the Marches, at Falkirk in 1298.[1] It was he who proclaimed on Christmas Day 1300 in Northampton Castle, in the presence of the king, the prohibition of tournaments in England.[2] Walter can safely be identified as le Roy Marchis who assisted at the Feast of the Swans. The career of a herald thus falls into line with that of many another seignorial official, as he proceeds from private to royal employment. This happened also to Mortimer's herald John O' the Lake in the fourteenth century.[3]

In 1306 as in 1290 the musicians and the heraldic experts are found side by side in the same list, but the personnel of the two departments may already have been distinct, a cleavage perhaps concealed by the conservatism of the records. The *Song of Caerlaverock* and the PRA exist side by side in the same manuscript, but they were not written by the same scribe, nor can they be attributed to the same author, for the one wrote in Anglo-Norman, but the *Song* is in Northern French.

It is possible, even probable, that the King's Heralds, like the King's Physicians or the Poet Laureate, were at all dates in private practice at the same time as they were employed by the king.

Other heralds at work in this period were John Butiler, Roger Machys (? for Marchys), and Thomas de Norff', to whom the king gave with his own hands on 6 April 1306 half a mark each for expenses in going between

---

[1] *Infra*, chap. VI. ii.
[2] Wagner, *Heralds and Heraldry*, p. 160. As Walter was paid 40s. for this, it is probable that he was responsible for the publication of the prohibition throughout the land.
[3] Wagner, op. cit., pp. 33, 35, 36.

Winchester and London:[1] and a considerable sum to two German minstrels employed at court for five years (1302–6).[2]

Later records show the persistence of this archaic classification. The two minstrels whose duty was 'to make minstrelsey before the king' are mentioned in the Ordinances of York of 1318[3] in the Marshal's department, but heralds as such are not mentioned. Sir Anthony Wagner has pointed out that even in 1332 John Teysaunt is variously described as *harald[us] domini Regis Anglie*, as one of fourteen *scutiferi et menestralli*, and as *menestrall[us] Regis*.[4] So it appears that the nomenclature used in the Pipe Rolls and even in the household books has lagged behind the facts. But rolls of arms such as the PRA were certainly drawn up by professional heralds and it would come as a surprise to find that the compilers also acted as minstrels, as apparently did the author of the *Song of Caerlaverock*. Edward I patronized both heralds and minstrels, but his son Edward of Caernarvon 'adhesit cantoribus, tragoediis etc.'[5] It seems a tenable view that the professions of herald and minstrel, long united, came to a parting of the ways in these years, and that the *Song of Caerlaverock* is a *tour de force*, combining perhaps for the last recorded time the expertise of both.

b. Heralds and Escheators

The earliest clear allusion to Norroy is in a release and quit-claim by Peter of 'bur' to Sir John son of Sir Ralph of Horbury[6] for 20 marks of silver (£13. 6s. 8d.) in payment of all debts from the beginning of the world to

[1] PRO (Exch. Acct. K.R.) 369/11, fol. 100 (Droxford's book).

[2] Ibid., fol. 102ᵛ. 'Henrico et Gunrado gigatoribus regis et menestrallis de Alemannia morantibus in Curia per preceptum regis pro menestralcia sua facienda etc. £12. 18s. 8d.'

[3] T. F. Tout, *The Place of Edward II in English History*, 2nd ed., p. 272, where these household ordinances are printed in full.

[4] Op. cit., p. 160.

[5] *Chron. Ed. I & II* (RS), ii. 91.

[6] Brit. Mus., Harl. Ch. 54 g. 44.

18 March 1276 (? 1277). The seal attached to the original bears three crowns upon a shield, but these are
crowns of office as a herald king and give no clue to his
identity.[1] He is described as 'King of Arms this side of
Trent *ex parte boreali*'. This way of locating places in the
middle ages is a peculiarity of royal documents. It refers
to the provinces (at that time) of the escheators, and it is
common knowledge that the *citra* or *ultra* is to be inter-
preted with reference to the situation of the writer at the
time. This charter clarifies the phrase beyond all doubt by
describing the herald's province as North of Trent, so that
he can be none other than Norroy thus mentioned in a
deed drawn up North of Trent.[2]

As the household roll of 1285 shows only two Kings of
Arms, it is reasonable to assume that one is for North and
the other South of Trent, as might be expected. For the
king's demesne and lands that fell in were divided in this
way, and the escheators who looked after them were at all
times not merely royal appointees, like the sheriffs, but
king's clerks closely associated, like the heralds, with the
royal household.

The coincidence of the escheatries with the provinces of
the heralds may be the clue to the composition and orderly
arrangement of the PRA. The escheators had great powers
and until the Ordainers in 1311 decided that they should
be appointed in Parliament, they were household men,
through whom the king (or Piers Gaveston as Regent)
controlled the wardships and marriages as they fell in. The
provinces were changed from time to time as it suited the
king, and in 1324, after Thomas of Lancaster's death,
the counties were rearranged to include in one province
the shires in which 'Lancaster' was prominent.[3]

---

[1] Wagner, *Heralds and Heraldry*, pp. 32, 39.

[2] Horbury is three miles SSW. of Wakefield in Yorkshire. John of Horbury is
PRA, no. 738 (Yorks.), and no. 227 on the Camden roll.

[3] Henry de Bray of Harleston (*c.* 1289–1340), Northants., was a typical
escheator. See his unique *Estate Book*, edited for the Camden Society in 1916 by
Miss Dorothy Wills. Mr. John Walwayn, who became Treasurer of England,

c. The Camden Roll

Though the Camden Roll[1] is not beautiful to look at, it is important in its own right as one of the few surviving original painted rolls of the thirteenth century, with French blazon of rather later date, it is said, on the dorse. The names of the bearers are, as in the Dering Roll, placed over the shields, of which there are 270 in 45 rows of 6. If the blazon is admitted to be French, it could be contemporary with the painting, as thirteenth-century northern French hands of this type are more advanced in appearance than English hands of the same date, from which they are not otherwise easily distinguishable. The roll was drawn up about 1280 and is the only one to contain 'Sire Aunfons' or Alfonso, eldest son of Edward I (no. 26) (born 24 November 1273, died August 1284), who had a household of his own of which fragmentary accounts remain.[2] A point of interest is that Alfonso had a coat of arms assigned to him as a child, though he did not live to be knighted. This is true also of Edmund of Woodstock (born 5 August 1301), for whom an armorial seal was made in 1303.[3]

This raises a considerable issue: whether at this date persons not of royal blood were entitled to use their inherited coats, if necessary with a suitable difference, before they were knighted.[4]

was another. See 'The Authorship of the *Vita Edwardi Secundi*', in *EHR* (1956), by the present author.

[1] Now Cottonian Roll xv. 8 in the British Museum. The roll has been printed in *Notes and Queries*, 6th ser., viii (1883), 21–23, 41–43, 83–85. See further *CEMRA*, pp. 18–19, but read '1883' as above for '1890'.

[2] Pipe Roll no. 130 (A.D. 1285), m. 5, an account from 20 November 1282 to 20 August 1284, and of Alfonso's household until its dispersion on 18 October 1284. See Hilda Johnstone, 'The Wardrobe and Household of the Sons of Edward I', in *Bull. Inst. Hist. Res.*, vol. ii, no. 5, p. 44, note 2.

[3] Johnstone, op. cit., citing PRO Exch. Accts. 363/14. It was made by a herald painter who came from London.

[4] Edward of Caernarvon, specifically nominated as Edward I's successor in 1297 when fealty was sworn to him (Vincent, *Lancashire Lay Subsidies*, pp. 200–1), has arms as 'filius Regis' on Collins' Roll when about 11, and as an

Among the foreigners are found the King of *Griffonie* and the King of *Bealme*, who may be fabulous. The King of Armenia on the other hand had recently sent envoys to England.[1] The 'Prince de Galles' (Llewelyn) is here but no other Welshmen. Most of the English and three Scottish earls (Angus, Athol, and Carrick) are given. Many of the forty or so foreign knights come from Flanders or northern France. The earls and counts are scattered *passim* in the roll, which is in no sort of order.[2]

Yet the roll with its French blazon may reflect some interest in the visit of the king and queen to Paris on 11 May 1279. The king had been with Llewelyn, still entitled, after the Treaty of Conway, Prince of Wales, at Rhuddlan in September 1278, and on 13 October Llewelyn married Eleanor de Montfort in Edward's presence at Worcester. In September, too, had taken place the great Round Table at Kenilworth. On 23 May 1279 the Treaty of Amiens was sealed with France and on 19 June the king landed again at Dover. It is not said that Alfonso, who was only five, accompanied his parents. He probably remained at King's Langley.

esquire at Caerlaverock at the age of 17. He bore his father's arms with a blue label.

¹ *CPR* (28 May 1278), p. 265. Safe-conduct for Armenian envoys lately come and now returning.

² Segar's Roll (*c.* 1282), of 212 names, is a like composition, beginning with Prester John, King of Jerusalem, King of Constantinople. It has been edited by J. Greenstreet in *The Genealogist*, iv (1880), 50–58, 90–97.

IV

THE DERING ROLL

THE Dering Roll, the property of Sir Anthony Wagner, Garter, is the finest of the extant Edwardian rolls and in every respect a document of great historical interest. The roll may be acephalous, for at this date general rolls may be expected to begin with the king followed by an impressive list of earls. The Dering Roll contains neither king, prince, nor earl, but begins with two royal bastards. In all there are five of John's natural children upon the roll. This seems excessive, unless there was some design on King John's part to associate them with Kent and Sussex, with which many of the knights are associated. This roll of 324 names, of whom seventy-eight are barons holding *inter alia* lands in Kent and Sussex, includes a number of sheriffs of Kent and four Constables of Dover Castle. By a sixteenth-century tradition current among the heralds and recorded by Ralph Brooke, the roll was associated with the siege of a castle by Edward I. Acre and Berwick were mentioned.[1] But by its contents the roll can be closely related to the rota system for castle-guard at Dover, and as it came into the possession of Sir Edward Dering in the seventeenth century, it is likely that he acquired it along with much other record material by abstracting it from the archives of the Castle. This view was arrived at after a detailed comparison of the Roll with the known details of the castle-guard system.[2]

Apart from its remarkable local concentration of tenants-in-chief—a quarter of the baronage—and the large number of knights who held part of their estate of the king in chief, the roll begins in a distinctive way with Richard

[1] *CEMRA*, p. 15.   [2] *Infra*, pp. 65–69.

Fitz Roy and William de Say, natural sons of King John, whose lands point at once to Dover Castle. They represent two of the nine 'custodies' into which the lands owing castle-guard to Dover were divided. As the roll is checked name by name, other custodies emerge. The roll might be described as a roll of the garrison as afforced from time to time in emergency. But it is as remarkable for its omissions as for its contents.

The Dering Roll could not have been completed before 1277–8.[1] If it is based upon a castle-guard roll made in the early years of Stephen of Penchester's term of office as Constable of Dover (1268–99) many of the anomalies and difficulties that it presents can be explained. It could have found a place in a *feodarium* or rental made at the time that Penchester, as the *History of Dover Castle* tells us, had the muniments arranged.

The tenurial liability for castle-guard may by 1275 be supposed to have been split up in some instances and accumulated in others. It is exceedingly difficult to trace. A medieval feodary or rental often gave, as it were, an address to apply to rather than the name of the actual tenant. Though everyone knew that X was dead, it was X's name that was on the rental, and to his address that the feodary applied for scutage or castle-guard money, so that a new rental usually incorporated the names of persons long dead.[2] Thus one feature of the Dering Roll can be paralleled in a Shropshire scutage roll of about the same date (1279–80). Bogo de Knoville, the sheriff, made his list entirely from old lists of Henry III. 'He named the tenants who held the fiefs under Henry III as if they

---

[1] Roger la Warre could not use his father's arms without a label until May 1277 (no. 103), Richard Fitz Thomas (no. 172) succeeded in 1275, William Peyferer (no. 67) in 1277, Alan la Zouche (no. 177) *d.* 1270. John de Balum (no. 159), the second baron, *d.* 1275, leaving Walter his son aged 50. Walter de Balum (perhaps John's father) *d.* 1245, being (according to Matt. Par., *Chron. Maj., s.a.* 1245) a brother of Osbert Giffard.

[2] This feature of rentals was frequently observed by the present writer when working on the archives of some Oxford colleges.

owed the money to Edward I and made no allowance for the actual service of several present tenants.' Thus he notes that £10 is due from five fees of Thomas Corbet, who was alive and had paid in 1235. Peter Corbet, a very active soldier, who served in 1277, is omitted.[1]

A castle-guard list has the additional complication that it cuts across a number of honours and baronies whose fees were for most purposes orientated towards another centre—its *caput*, e.g. the Constable's honour of Haughley had its *caput* at Haughley, not Dover.

If the list is not acephalous, No. 1, Richard Fitz Roy, may be regarded as its hero. Penchester was old enough to have known him before he died, and the handwriting, which looks, as often in Rolls of Arms, deliberately archaic, would be appropriate in a script of that date, though the roll was actually written a generation later.

The list is not, however, entirely one of persons who *owed* castle-guard to Dover, but it may well include many who *habitually performed that service as deputies* for men who owed it. They would naturally be men to whom it was convenient, men who had lands in Kent and Sussex, not unwilling to do their military service in a garrison town. It may be this that gives the Roll its curiously selective look.

The chief link between the Dering Roll and Dover Castle is the appearance on the roll of the holders of custodies as follows:

Custody No. I   Stephen of Penchester (no. 6).
    II   Ralph of Sandwich (no. 10), heir of Avranches.
   III   The heirs of Robert and Fulbert of Dover may account for some of the foreigners.
   IV   Richard de Gray (no. 209) and Bernard de Gray (no. 206), heirs of Manasser Arsic.
   V   Richard Fitz Rey (no. 1).
   VI   William de Say (no. 2), Maminot custody.
  VII   John de St. John (no. 91), heir of Port of Basing.

---

[1] J. E. Morris, *The Welsh Wars of Edward I* (1901), pp. 37–38.

VIII Robert de Crevequer (no. 3).

IX The Fitzwilliam custody. As FitzWilliam lost his estates in 1075 the descent is obscure,[1] but the estates should be in Herefordshire or the West as his father William FitzOsbern was Earl of Hereford. If the history of the Castle is reliable the custodies as reported must have been organized between 1071 and 1075, otherwise the name Fitzwilliam custody would have no significance.

A score of other links, formed by the occurrence in the roll of persons known to have owed castle-guard to Dover, are noted below and help to strengthen this hypothesis.

There were nine custodies at Dover, but the rota of knights for castle-guard was provided from eight, the Constable—perhaps only in theory—being always in residence. The celebrated forty days' period of feudal service[2] has no place in the rota, which is known from Dugdale's use of the 'Quire of Dover' and Penchester's feodary as used in the *History of Dover Castle*. The rota was based on periods of four weeks, as at Hastings, making thirteen lunar months in the year.

Castle-guard was due from the 169 or 170 fees that made up the nine baronies. In 1274 it was worth £146, presumably the sum collected by the feodary. But castle-guard could be done in person, by deputy, or by payment of a fixed sum. Already in 1215 the barons complained that they were being distrained to pay even if they had performed the service in person.[3] The sheriffs were collecting a fixed annual sum on all fees that owed the service,

---

[1] There is a Thomas Fitz William who as no. 132 on Glover's Roll (ed. Nicoles) bears *Masculy d'Ermine et de Goules,* this being also the coat assigned to Richard de la Rokele (no. 131). For a possible line of research see C. A. F. Meekings, 'Adam FitzWilliam (d. 1238)', in *BIHR,* May 1961, 1–15. This Adam was a Herefordshire knight whose chief seat was at Hatfield. The family connexion with Kent was 'practically severed' in 1252; and there is no Hereford connexion.

[2] For the forty-day period see 'The Significance of Scutage Rates in Eleventh- and Twelfth-Century England', by C. Warren Hollister in *EHR* lxxv (Oct. 1960).

[3] See the 'Articles of the Barons', art. 19, and the Charter of 121, art. 29 and its reissues.

and these dues, like the scutage, were being passed on to sub-tenants and paid on small fractions of a fee. The normal rate shown in the *Inquisitiones post mortem* was 10*s.* a fee, but this would only produce £89—which, when the castle was built and knights paid 6*d.* a day,[1] would provide for the garrison. But from *c.* 1175, at 2*s.* a day per knight, the ten knights would cost £365 a year or £400 if the Constable was paid double as a banneret.[2] Much useful information on castle-guard has been brought together by Professor Sidney Painter,[3] but for Dover Mr. Painter has misunderstood the evidence. Mr. Painter states that the fifty-six fees of the Honour of Haughley—the Constable's honour—were divided into thirteen groups of four or five each marked *unum mensem*[4] and comments, 'on this basis the Constable's barony alone would supply a permanent garrison of four or five knights each serving a month of four weeks'. This is not so. The Constable's Honour of Haughley provided only the Constable, and the groups of four or five are not the *knights provided* but the Haughley *tenants responsible* month by month for paying the wages of the Constable (? or his deputy), who alone is permanent. This at once reduces the total garrison from a total of twenty-two or twenty-three to seventeen or eighteen, and the further reduction to ten is necessary by Mr. Painter's misunderstanding of the rota system by which the service of the remaining eight baronies was arranged. These eight baronies provided 117 men for service each year, and their rotation, though complicated, can be known. The nine baronies comprised 169/170

---

[1] In 1162–3 '7 milites soldariorum de toto anno' cost £80. 18*s.* 8*d.*, and 20 sergeants £30. 6*s.* 8*d.*, eight arbalisterii £80. 16*s.* 0*d.* (*Pipe Roll*, 8 Hen. II, p. 53). On the other hand knights and sergeants together cost only £75. 0*s.* 7*d.* in 1160/1 (*Pipe Roll*, 7 Hen. II, p. 61).

[2] The balance was made up in practice out of the customs and tolls of the port of Dover. The jump in payment of knights is very sudden and needs investigation.

[3] *American Hist. Rev.* xl (1935), 450–9, 'Castle-Guard', by S. Painter. Useful also for Richmond, Windsor, and Devizes and commutation rates in general.

[4] *Red Book of the Exchequer*, pp. 706–12.

fees of which Haughley comprised fifty-six. The remaining (?) 114 fees of eight baronies provided in the course of one year a total of 117 knights who appear in person or by deputy in a traditional rota, producing a garrison of nine knights plus the Constable. There is no provision in these arrangements for expansion of the garrison in time of war.[1]

In 1268 Edward took the Cross in June at Northampton, and the Papal Legate Ottobuoni left the country.[2] By arrangements begun late in November at Winchester, Edward became Steward of England and, at Christmas, Warden of London. He was also granted the custody of all the royal castles in England for a period of five years.[3] He or his agents, not the king, appointed the sheriffs during this period. Edward had become the uncrowned king of England, leaving his father Henry III as only a figurehead.

Edward left in charge a group of four men, William Gifford, the Archbishop of York, Philip Basset, Roger Mortimer, and his private chancellor, Robert Burnell, whom he hoped to impose upon the monks of Canterbury as Archbishop. From the death of Henry III in 1272 until Edward's return in 1274 these men, under Richard of Cornwall, were to act as a Council of Regency. Edward had thus in 1265–6 managed to concentrate in his own hands the military key-points of the country, and before he went on Crusade had achieved the position held by Earl Simon between Lewes and Evesham, being king in all but name. For the grant of the castles altered the balance of political power for him personally almost as much as their resumption by Hubert de Burgh in 1223.[4] The arrangements for the safe keeping of these castles are

---

[1] Such a provision is, however, found at Devizes (Painter, 458–9).

[2] *Supra*, p. 46.

[3] *CPR*, p. 507; *Ann. Wint.* (RS), p. 107.

[4] Dr. W. A. Morris in *The Medieval English Sheriff to 1300* (Manchester, 1927) omitted to use the evidence of the whole volume of *CPR* (1266–72), though he used earlier and later volumes extensively. This did not attract the attention of reviewers (e.g. *EHR* (1928), pp. 99–101).

known from retrospective entries on the Patent Roll for
1270, covering sixteen counties, when there was a change
of castellans consequent upon Edward's departure, and
some later appointments by his agents can be traced in the
Public Record Office *List of Sheriffs*.[1]

Dover Castle, which Edward had captured, was granted
to him with Scarborough, Bamburgh, Nottingham, and
Corfe at Winchester in November 1265, three months
after the Battle of Evesham. Edward thus possessed himself of the Key to England, which even in 1253 some had
feared he might snatch before his time—he was then only
fourteen.[2] His commission of the Tower to Philip Basset[3]
and Dover Castle to Stephen of Penchester was confirmed
before he left England on 20 August 1270.[4] It is also
relevant to our theme to note that King Henry, *after con-
sultation with Edward*, admitted Roger Bigod, nephew of
Earl Roger, as Marshal.[5]

Earl Richard of Cornwall, King of the Romans, was
left in charge of Edward's children and estates, and the
four councillors were to be under him. If anything happened to Henry III, Richard was to take Edward's place,
and failing him Henry of Almain, and failing him the four
were to choose a 'sovereyn' until the full age (which was to
be twenty) of the heirs. If Henry died the five of them
were to guard all the issues of England.[6] The quarrel with
Gloucester was patched up and the Earl promised to go
with 'the next passage', but he failed to do so.[7] That

[1] The counties named are Beds. and Berks., Camb., Essex and Herts., Kent,
Oxford and Bucks., Norf. and Suff., Notts. and Derby, Salop and Staffs. See
CPR (1258–66), p. 645; (1266–72), pp. 91, 468–72, 508, 509, 536, 659.

[2] *Foed.*, p. 292 (20 July 1253), *CPR*, p. 214.

[3] *CPR*, p. 453 (10 August 1270).

[4] Financially he was made secure by the grant of the Customs of Bordeaux,
the English Customs, and the New Aid, all of which he farmed to Italian
merchants (*CPR*, pp. 42, 396, 442, 630). These helped to eke out the income from
his appanage which included the profits of Gascony—if there were any after
deducting the customs—Ireland, and Bristol Castle, where he had, initially, his
Exchequer.   [5] *Cl. R.*, p. 264 (4 May 1270 at Westminster).

[6] *Foed.*, p. 484, from 'Liber A', an Anglo-Norman chirograph.

[7] F. M. Powicke, *Henry III and the Lord Edward*, p. 579.

Richard of Cornwall was effectively Regent early in 1271
is shown by a dispute between Dover Priory and the
Official of Canterbury heard before him at Wallingford in
the presence of six or seven bishops. The chronicler states
that Richard gave his decision *in virtute regia, qua vice
fratris sui fungebatur.*[1]

This then is the political background to the first three
years of Stephen of Penchester's long term of office as
Constable of Dover. The man put in charge at such a
time must surely have shown personal qualities of which
we know nothing, and for which there is not a scrap
of evidence on which to base a guess, but there is good
reason to believe that he found favour at Court for family
reasons.

(1) STEPHEN OF PENCHESTER, CONSTABLE OF DOVER

The manor of Penshurst or Penchester by Ashburnham is
described as the chief seat of the 'old Kentish family' from
which Stephen sprang. It was held in the later years of
Henry III's reign by John de Bellemains, a canon of St.
Paul's, who was Stephen's uncle and trustee.[2] The place
is near Hastings, four miles west of Battle. Penchester
comes to light on 21 May 1267 when he was with the
Lord Edward in some private transaction at Sandwich.
His status in this is not clear, but he may have already
become a member of Edward's household.[3] Next year on
20 November, a few months after Edward had taken the
Cross, Penchester was made Constable of Dover, Sheriff
of Kent, and Warden of the Cinque Ports.[4] As Warden of

---

[1] *Gervase of Canterbury*, ii. 257.

[2] *DNB* art. Penchester by T. F. T[out]. I have not found his *IPM*.

[3] *Sir Christopher Hatton's 'Book of Seals'*, edited for the Northampton Rec.
Soc. as no. 94 by the late Lewis C. Lloyd and Doris Mary Stenton.

[4] *CPR*, p. 186, *Gerv. Cant.* ii. 246 (A.D. 1268). For the form of the name Pene-
hurst, or Penc-, or Pens-, see *Place Names of Sussex*, Part II (1930), ed. A. Mawer
and F. M. Stenton with E. B. Gover.

the Cinque Ports Penchester had also the final responsibility for the customs and the 'passage' money. It is not
said whether this covered the cross-channel fare, which in
1285 varied (it may be supposed according to the amount
of luggage or 'harness') from 2*d*. to 4*d*. for a man and 6*d*.
to 10*d*. for a horse.[1] He remained Sheriff only until 1271,
but he was Constable until his death in 1299.[2] From time
to time Stephen acted as a Judge of Oyer et Terminer,
and in and after 1283 he helped to lay out New Winchelsea, but he never appears as a 'strenuous knight'. In 1278
Penchester and his wife Margaret were sent to Castile to
fetch Joan, daughter of Edward I, who was being educated
there.[3] It was intended that she should marry Hartman,
son of Rudolph of Habsburg, but Rudolph died in 1282.

A clue to Penchester's sudden advancement from local
obscurity to high office may possibly be found in his coat
of arms, for he bore the same charge upon his shield as
Peter of Savoy, the Queen's uncle.

(ii) PENCHESTER AND CASTLE-GUARD

Though Penchester is so much associated with Dover,
he was actually a tenant of the Honour of Hastings in
Sussex. The castle, rape, and honour of Hastings had a
complicated history but were held alternately by Peter of
Savoy and the Lord Edward between 1249 and 1268.

The rape and barony of Hastings, the one-time honour
of the Count of Eu, was a highly privileged liberty with
its own sheriff. Castle-guard to Hastings was shared
between four wards in each of which fifteen tenants had

---

[1] *Foed.* (12 June 1285), p. 659.

[2] Stephen is said to have held the seven hundreds of the Weald formerly held
by Roger de Leyburne, who d. 1271 (*Exc. et Rot. Fin.* ii. 552). He probably
enlarged his jurisdiction at the Castle. Cap. VI of the *Articuli super Cartas* says
of Pleas of Dover Castle that none be allowed, save it touch *la garde du chestel*,
and there was an article at Stamford (1309) against King's Constables taking
cognizance of Common Pleas.

[3] *Foed.*, p. 559, *ex orig.*

successively to serve the castle lunar month by lunar month. The knights of Fairbright Ward took the first month, those of Wastling the second, those of Warbleton the third, and those of Etchingham the fourth. The service from any particular fee came seven times in two years.[1] Here as at Dover, the rate of commutation did not suffice to replace the service,[2] and this, as Mr. Painter has already observed, is likely to be so because garrison duty is normally less onerous than fighting the Welsh or Scots, or serving in Ireland or France.

Peter of Savoy came to England as a result of Henry III's marriage in January 1236 to Eleanor of Provence. He arrived in 1241 and was knighted at Christmas, and given the honour but not the earldom of Richmond. He proposed a tournament *à outrance* with Roger Bigod— foreigners against the English, to be held at Northampton. This Henry III encouraged until he realized that his friends were likely to get the worst of it, when he pro- hibited the meeting.[3] Now Peter of Savoy had charge of Kent in the first half of 1241, until Bertram de Crioil succeeded him. The date, the place, *the identity of arms*, the sudden emergence of Stephen on the death of Peter, all combine to suggest the possibility that Stephen of Penchester was a natural son of the Count, and could, when Peter of Savoy died abroad in May 1268 without male heirs,[4] assume his father's arms without a difference

---

[1] *VCH Sussex*, ix (1937), 1–2. The arrangements for castle-guard at Hastings are given in *Red Book of the Exchequer*, pp. 622–3, and *Cal. IPM*, vii, no. 247.

[2] For further information see Painter, op. cit., p. 456.

[3] Matt. Par., *Chron. Maj.* iv. 88. One was held in June 1241 at Hertford which resulted in the death of Gilbert Marshal, Earl of Pembroke, a man of small stature, intended for Holy Orders. He was riding an Italian charger which was too high-spirited for him. The bridle broke and the horse threw its head violently backwards, striking him in the chest and hurling him from the saddle. He was carried to a monastery and died that night. Others, too, were killed in that tournament. (Paris, iv. 135; *Wav.*, p. 338.)

[4] Peter of Savoy returned home to become count in 1263. Edward released to him the castle and honour of Hastings on 18 September 1262, and on his death granted it to Peter's successor in the honour of Richmond, John of Brittany (*CPR*, 1266–72, pp. 375, 733). *Royal Letters* (Rolls Series), ii. 211.

as Constable of Dover in that year. After twenty years' familiarity with the Count this identity of arms could not have passed unnoticed by Edward. Unless there had been a reason, would he have permitted this assumption of such a coat by someone in so public an office?

Penchester would have been up to five years old perhaps when Richard Fitz Roy died in 1242, if this suggestion about his parentage is correct, and could have heard about the French prisoners at Dover,[1] after the sea-fight off Sandwich in 1217, in which Richard took part, from Richard himself.

The knight's fees owing castle-guard to Dover numbered 168/170, according to the twelfth- and thirteenth-century lists in the *Red Book of the Exchequer*, divided into nine custodies, to share the burden of guarding the castle for thirteen periods of four weeks between the nine knights and the Constable who formed the garrison. These fees are scattered and represent the way in which the barons originally responsible for the service had territorialized their burden: they throw little light on service actually performed. To track this down we have to cast back from a later account of how the duty of castle-guard was arranged within the castle. In Alexander Campbell's translation of William Darell's authoritative work on Dover Castle it is stated that 'By his [Stephen of Penchester's] orders all the records of the castle, all the writings and instruments granted to the Constable, were collected together into a book, which he called the castle's charter-book.'[2] It seems to be from this source too that Campbell

---

[1] *Hist. de Guillaume le Maréchal*, ed. Paul Meyer, II, 17572–76. The form of entry 'Le Sire de *X*' towards the end of the roll can in some cases mean merely that the herald-painter was unaware of *Monsieur un tel*'s christian name, and in a French-speaking country a man is not necessarily a foreigner because he is so described. The actual foreigners are not so numerous as appear at first sight. Some may be connected with the foreign service originally due to the barony of Dover (Dugdale, *Bar.*, p. 481).

[2] *The History of Dover Castle*, by Alexander Campbell (1786–97), being a partial translation of a Latin work, now in the College of Arms, by William Darell, p. 46.

took his unique account of the arrangements for castle-guard. The book is likely to have been removed from the castle, together with the Dering Roll of Arms, by Sir Edward Dering at the time when he removed its charters.[1]

In Campbell's translation of Darell's book the precise arrangements for castle-guard by the knights of the nine custodies are clearly set forth.[2] The Constable's does not come into the rotation as he was, in theory it may be supposed, always in residence. The other eight custodies provided between them a sufficient number of knights to maintain a resident garrison of nine knights who each served for four weeks, except in the case of Fitz William whose three knights served for two months every year, possibly because they had to travel so far that a shorter stay was uneconomical. Robert or Hugh Crevequer sent five knights, all of them to guard the castle for twenty-six weeks, but after two months two of them were allowed to depart. This, at any rate, was the tradition received by Campbell.

The year being lunar, not the calendar year, the castle-guard falls into thirteen periods each of four weeks, divided between custodies I–VIII as follows:

Period			
1	Avranches (II) 3 kts. × 7 periods of duty = 21 kts. (*Dering Roll 10*)	Dover (III)* 3 kts. × 5 periods of duty = 15 kts.	Peverel (V) *or* Chilham 3 kts. × 6 periods of duty = 18 kts.
2			
3			
4			

* Cited by Dugdale in his *Baronage*, i. 461, from *Le Quire de Dover* in the Exchequer, as in Lambarde's *Perambulation of Kent*, pp. 304, 315. This *Quire de Dover* has not yet been found by me.

[1] The evidence for Sir Edward Dering's removal of the charters from Dover is given by C. E. Wright in 'Sir Edward Dering; a seventeenth-century Antiquary and his Saxon charters', in *The Early Cultures of North West Europe*, ed. C. Fox and B. Dickins (Cambridge, 1950), pp. 369–93. I owe this reference to Sir Anthony Wagner.

[2] Op. cit., pp. 19 ff.

Period

5
6

Maminot (VI)
3 kts. × 8 periods
of duty = 24 kts.

FitzWilliam (IX)
3 kts. × 2 periods
of duty = 6 kts.

7

8   Arsic (IV)
3 kts. × 6 periods
of duty = 18 kts.

9

{ Crevequer (VIII)† }
{ Port (VII) *or* Basing }
or St. John
(*Dering no.* 91)

10
11
12
13

† Port sent 12 kts. 2 at a time, covering 6 periods. Crevequer sent 3 kts. for 26 weeks covering 6½ periods, but after 2 months 2 were allowed to depart. Thus a very slight over-provision seems to be made.

The rotation thus provides 9 knights at a time for 8 custodies, or 114 knights every year.

The needs of the castle were thus served by 117 knights in one calendar year, or nine a month for thirteen lunar months. If they served a period of fifteen years each— which is thought to be a fair average for the working life of a strenuous knight—there would be a complete turnover 2½ times in 37½ years—the period apparently covered by the roll—1240–1277/8. This would result in 292½ knights plus the Constable and the foreigners, which would raise the total to the 324 names actually found upon the roll. It is probable that the men of Kent and Sussex would find it convenient and possibly not un-pleasant to pass a portion of every year in Dover Castle either as persons owing the service or as local deputies for those who lived further afield. The king and his earls had no part in this castle-guard service, and are not on the roll. It may not have been thus, but this has proved a working hypothesis.

a. Note on Licensed Castles

There were some 170 barons in William the Conqueror's reign and 169 bannerets in the PRA.[1] A like number of private castles might therefore be expected. Mr. Painter has indeed counted a total of 209 castles in King John's reign, but there was an implicit theory that private castles existed only on sufferance, a theory that is made explicit in the thirteenth century, when licences to crenellate a dwelling were sought and granted in considerable numbers. From time to time 'adulterine' castle were destroyed and others were rased because their owners rebelled, e.g. Skipsea. Under Hubert de Burgh, when royal authority had to be reasserted after the civil wars of John's reign, there was in 1223–4 a wholesale resumption, or taking into the king's hands, of many castles where castellans once appointed by John had entrenched themselves as if by prescriptive right. At times they threatened the security of the country-side and the structure of royal administration, as did the notorious Falkes de Breauté at Bedford and other castles.

b. Note on Licences to Crenellate

In 1271 Penchester had licence to crenellate—that is to embattle—his house 'like a castle' at Hever in Kent (*CPR*, 1266–72, p. 507), and ten years later (25 May 1281) he and Margaret his wife had the like for their (? small) house of Allington in Kent (*CPR*, 1272–81, p. 437). Walter Langton, perhaps reflecting upon his own unpopularity, had at least five licences between 1299 and 1306: (i) for his house and the canons' houses in the close at Lichfield (*CPR*, 1299, p. 409); (ii) for a private house at Thorp Watervill in Northants. (*CPR*, 1301, p. 561); (iii) for his London house outside Temple Bar and in his Bishopric (*CPR*, p. 367, 19 June 1305); (iv) for the houses he was building at Beaudesert and Ashley David

---

[1] A few at the end of the PRA list are fifteenth-century additions.

or elsewhere, 'wherever he pleases' (*CPR*, p. 462, 16 Sept. 1306); and (v) again for the close at Lichfield (*CPR*, p. 463, 4 Oct. 1306). There are about another twenty-five such licences to private persons between 1290 and 1307.

A William de Hever bearing Penchester's arms with a blue label is no. 201 on Camden's Roll, so presumably a son who *fl.* 1280.

(iii) THE CUSTODIES OF DOVER

1. *The Custody of the Constable.* The barony of Haughley in Essex consisted of 56½ fees in '1261–2'.[1] It was held by the Montfort family under Henry I, who had four constables each coming to court for three months 'and charged respectively with the castles of Dover, Oxford, Worcester, and Gloucester'. These offices were hereditary in the families of Montfort, D'Oilli, D'Abitot, and Gloucester.[2] Dover descended from Robert de Vere through Adeline de Montfort, his wife, to Henry of Essex who forfeited it in 1163. The Montfort family are nos. 83, 163 on the roll.

From 1223 to 1232 Hubert de Burgh held it with the earldom of Kent, and received £1,000 a year for it.[3] The actual custody was deputed to Robert de Nereford in 1244.[4] From 1232 to 1255 Bertram de Crioil, a baron, was Constable of Dover and Warden of the Cinque Ports and Sheriff of Kent. He was succeeded by Reginald de Cobham (1255) and Nicholas de Molis (6 Jan. 1258), followed by Richard de Grey, the 'baronial' nominee

---

[1] The number of knight's fees is given in two lists, one headed '1261–2' (*for* 1161–2 ?) in the *Red Book of the Exchequer* (RS), ii. 613–19, 717–22, and these tally more or less with the evidence in the *History of Dover Castle*. Cf. *Book of Fees*, pp. 1457 ff.

[2] *Dialogus de Scaccario*, ed. Charles Johnson, in Nelson's Medieval Latin Classics (1950), p. xxxii.

[3] *R. lit. cl.*, p. 545a.

[4] Ibid., pp. 622, 625a

(1258–63), and in 1265 we find Geoffrey de Neville and Matthew de Bezillis.[1]

From 18 October 1265 the castle was directly under the control of the Lord Edward, who on 30 January 1268 in parliament at London appointed Stephen of Penchester (alias Penshurst), who remained in office until his death in 1299.[2]

The state of the castle comes to light in 1232, when it was committed to Bertram de Crioil, a baron, with the issues of the port, the toll of the town of Dover, the castle-wards, and, in addition, 300 marks a year. From these sources he had to pay the ten knights, five mounted ser-geants (*servientes equites*), five mounted slingers, five foot slingers, twenty watchmen (*vigiles*), one janitor, two smiths, one mason, one keeper of the *garnistura*, and to find food for the recluse.[3] When the king went to Gascony in 1242 Crioil guaranteed the safety of Dover, Canterbury, and Rochester castles,[4] and the men of Sussex, Surrey, Kent, and Essex were to be 'intendent' to him.[5]

The castle was perhaps unique in having no demesne of its own: for its whole sustenance it battened upon the surrounding country-side, taking a fixed sum from each of the nine constituent baronies of the Castle Honour (if it was ever so called), while they in other respects lived their own lives, with the usual complement of honour courts and knight-service.

The castle-guards were collected by a feodary or bailiff of fees, who was also in charge of the *garnistura*, and had to distrain the tenants of the houses in the castle to build and repair their houses. In the records he is called the Consta-ble's sergeant. It may be that the *garnistura* included the armoury, and that the feodary and his assistants (if any)

---

[1] *Gerv. Cant.* ii. 243. Apparently Matthew de Bezillis was left in charge after Evesham until he was deposed in parliament. [2] *CPR* (1268), p. 186.

[3] *Cl. R.* (1231–4), p. 154. The amount brought in by castle-guard rents is not stated. Crioil held the custody of Avranches (Honour of Folkestone) (*Rot. Hund.* i. 226). [4] *CPR* (7 April 1242), p. 1242.

[5] *CPR* (1 August 1242), p. 300.

repainted the shields when necessary, with some of the skill of a herald-painter. The man in charge of Penchester's feodary or book of fees in or after 1268 would be the successor of Robert Torneboel, a permanent resident at the castle for fifty years. When in 1255 the king, for the alleviation of the costs of keeping Dover Castle, caused the feeble and impotent surplus of the garrison to be removed, not willing that those should be in want so long as they lived who had done well in his service, he granted to Robert Torneboel, who from his first youth to decrepit old age did faithful service to King John and to the king, 100 shillings a year for life.[1]

So the castle had its feodary, who compiled the list of fees for the constable and, with the help of the sheriff, collected the castle-guard money. In 1256 Hugh de Lesseburn was appointed in this capacity as sergeant to Reginald de Cobham, the constable.[2] We hear of none other, so, if he was in office only half as long as his predecessor, it would have fallen to him to compile the list that Penchester had ordered to be made (c. 1268–77). It could have fallen to his lot also to paint the actual Roll of Arms now known as the Dering Roll. The handwriting is deliberately archaic, as frequently in heraldic documents, and is therefore no proof that the scribe had learned to write c. 1240–50. The suggestion made is that the man who actually painted the shields used in battle also copied them in miniature on to the Dering Roll. No scrap of evidence has been found to support this hazardous conclusion, but someone painted the roll, and it is possible that he gained experience as a herald painter by working upon solid metal shields.[3]

---

[1] CPR (1 Sept. 1255), p. 430.

[2] Ibid., p. 430 (8 June 1256).

[3] For years Lesseburn and Turneboel worked together, or alternately (Hugh in 1233, CPR, p. 12; Turneboel in 1240 and Hugh in 1242, ibid., pp. 239, 299). During a political crisis in 1242 Richard de Handlo, Gilbert de Ceriton, and Thomas Maunsel were appointed instead (ibid., p. 288). Lesseburn seems to be a generation younger than his colleague.

The rents collected by these feodaries bore no relation to the cost in the thirteenth century of providing a garrison of ten knights, plus the lesser folk. Sums due from knight's fees or fractions thereof crop up from time to time in the inquests held on the death of a tenant-in-chief or the tenant of an escheated barony, but they are only of use in pointing to outdated financial arrangements, and to the tenures upon which the responsibility lay of paying up or sending soldiers, an alternative which was open to the tenant. The old standard rate being ten shillings on the fee, the sum produced would be only £85.

In time of war the garrison could be increased enormously, as in the civil war that resulted from the invasion of England by Prince Louis of France in 1215. The next year the garrison is said to have numbered 140 knights in addition to the sergeants.[1] This great influx is partly explained by the long-existing links with north-eastern France and Flanders, and particularly by the provision from Robert of Dover's custody (no. 3) of knights from Normandy.[2] From the broader point of view, it is important that the Count of Flanders was himself an English stipendiary knight.[3]

In Flanders Richard I and John found an ally against Capetian encroachments and Capetian suzerainty. The 'Flemish mercenaries', as they are termed in the records, of these two kings came from Flanders, Brabant, Holland, Artois, and the districts bordering the Meuse. This is especially so after 1203, when Normandy was closed as a recruiting-ground for knights whom the king could attach to his personal service. These men are difficult to trace because they were paid by Exchequer fees in cash, and not often in fees of land.[4] Some of them, like Falkes

[1] Wendover, ii. 191, and *Histoire des Ducs*, p. 170, agree on this figure.
[2] Dugdale, *Baronage*, ii. 481.
[3] William of Malmesbury, *Gesta Regum* (RS), ii. 478–9.
[4] The Count of Holland undertook to send twenty-five knights (*Rot. Chart.*, pp. 190–1, of March 1213) and Waleran, son of the Duke of Limburg, ten knights (*Foed.* i, 106), but the bulk came singly or with one or two followers.

de Breauté, a Norman, or Engelard de Cigogné, starting as mere mercenaries, had long and—up to a point—distinguished careers in England as trusted household knights of the king.

Hugh de Boves (Dering Roll, no. 141) was one, a refugee from the French court,[1] and Ralph de Nele another. As Hugh died in 1215 his is one of the earliest names on the roll. A soldier of fortune, he became one of the most prominent and most hated of John's foreign officials,[2] in charge of recruiting foreign knights for the 'Army of Dover'—its contemporary official name—against the threatened invasion of 1213, when the Pope had enjoined Philip Augustus to conquer England. Recruiting had gone on steadily since the treaty of 1197 between Richard I and Count Baldwin of Flanders. Dover was the port of disembarkation and Hugh de Boves made it his headquarters.[3] He was granted the custody of the Pecché lands and so had almost the status of a baron.

It was the Chilham custody (no. 3), with its cross-channel interests, that had to do with the fighting at sea. Fitz Roy of Chilham led a ship or ships at the battle off Sandwich in 1217, where the French and Flemish knights who had invaded England with Prince Louis of France in 1215 were defeated and some captured. The rebels were also in the large-scale but almost bloodless 'Fair of Lincoln'. Some of the prisoners were imprisoned in Dover Castle (e.g. the Constable of Arras, no. 310 on the roll).[4]

The link with Flanders and north-east France was maintained in June 1267 when Flemish stipendiaries, including the Counts of St. Pol, Boulogne, and Guisnes,

---

[1] Wendover, ii. 109.

[2] Ibid., p. 105, where he is described as 'cruel and proud'.

[3] Hugh was at Dover 23 June 1215, just after Runnymede, and was told to send home those whom he had with him. He was shipwrecked and died on returning from Flanders, whither he had gone to raise mercenaries with whom John proposed to crush his rebellious barons (Wendover, ii. 147; Hist. des Ducs, ed. F. Michel (Paris, 1857), p. 157; R. lit. cl. i. 230b.

[4] F. M. Powicke, The Thirteenth Century, p. 11.

came with 100 knights and stayed for about a month with the king at Stamford.[1] They had been summoned by Roger de Leybourne to help Henry III (or the Lord Edward) repress Gloucester's rebellion.

Godfrey de Basevile of Buckinghamshire is included (no. 290) because he married Roysia, Penchester's daughter; Gerard de Rodes (no. 301) is a well-known English knight; and Baldwin de Guisnes (alias Guise) sold property to Hubert de Burgh in Kent. Baldwin de Betun, a Fleming, Count of Aumale, was also Lord of Holderness at Yorkshire.[2]

The Constables of Dover

1223   *Hubert de Burgh at £1,000 a year (R. lit. cl.,* p. 545[a]).
1224   Robert de Nereford (cf. Wm. de N. of Suffolk, *IPM*, 30 Ed. I, who is no. 282). Ibid., pp. 622, 625.
1232–55   *Bertram de Crioil.*[3]
1255–(occ. June 1256)   *Reginald de Cobham*   (Henry 'le Oncle' of Roundel, Kent, who married Penchester's daughter, is no. 15 and John de Cobham, Sheriff of Kent 1260–1, is no. 12.)
1258 (6 Jan.)   *Nicholas de Molis*, appointed by the magnates.
1258–16 Oct. 1263   *Richard de Grey*, 1258–?
1265   *Geoffrey de Neville.*
        Matthew de Bezillis.
1265 (18 Oct.)   The Lord Edward took the Castle.
1268 (Jan.)–1299   *Stephen of Penchester.*

The remaining Custodies, providing the rota of service, were:

2. *The Custody of* AVRANCHES (de Abrincis) or the 'manor' or 'honour' of Folkestone provided twenty-one knights. This was inherited by Crevequer (Custody no. 8) in 1236. It was described in 1278 as formerly shared by

---

[1] *Gerv. Cant.* ii. 246; Wykes, p. 204; *Ann. Lond.*, p. 78. Further, Ramsay, *Dawn*, p. 262.

[2] John de Betune is no. 322 on the roll.

[3] On 4 November 1241 Henry de Bohun, Earl of Essex and Hereford, surrendered the castle, which had been committed to him during pleasure. (*CPR*, p. 265.)

Bertram de Crioil (q.v.) and Nicholas of Sandwich, who each held seven fees.[1] (An untraced portion seems necessary here.)

3. *The Custody of Robert of* DOVER provided fifteen knights. These are the 14 + 1 fees of the honour of Fulbert of Dover in Kent.[2] Dugdale alludes also to lands in Normandy.[3] The marriage of Richard Fitz Roy to Roese of Dover presumably fused this custody with no. 5, thus producing very nearly the amount of castle-guard due according to Dugdale.

4. *The Custody of* ARSIC provided fifteen knights (*recte* 18). These came from the barony of Cogges by Witney in Oxfordshire, with twenty fees appurtenant. Held by the Bishop of Bayeux's tenant, Wodard, in 1086.[4] In 1166 Manasser Arsic had fourteen knights holding about 18 fees.[5] In 1212 Robert Arsic held $4\frac{1}{2}$ fees in Oxfordshire,[6] in which year King John gave the lands to Oxford Castle, after the rebellion of Robert.[7]

On the extinction of the line the remainder interest was granted by the heiresses to Walter Grey, Archbishop of York (*d.* 1255). Richard de Grey is no. 209 on the roll, and Bernard de Grey, bearing the same arms with a label, is no. 209. Robert de Grey held Ouresby in Lincolnshire in chief in 1276 and owed castle-guard to Dover.[8]

5. *The Custody of* PEVEREL [of Dover] = the barony of Chilham in Kent. Fifteen knights (*recte* 18 ?). Thomas Peverel held the barony 1213–16, and Richard Fitz Roy (no. 1) 1216–45. Thomas Peverel, perhaps a grandson, who was aged thirty in 1276, is no. 115. The barony

---

[1] *Rot. Hund.* i. 226.   [2] *Book of Fees*, p. 569.

[3] Dugdale, *Baronage*, i. 481. See also *Book of Fees* (A.D. 1242), pp. 656, 660, 661: 269, 590, 675.

[4] D.B., i, fols. 154–6.   [5] *Red Book of the Exchequer*, 302–5.

[6] *Book of Fees*, i. 102.

[7] See Dugdale, *Bar.* i. 538, for the pedigree and I. J. Sanders, *Feudal Military Service in England* (1956), p. 155, note 1.

[8] *Rot. Hund.* i. 360.

passed to Alexander de Balliol (b. about 1258), of Cavers, who was still employed by Edward II (*Song of Caerlaverock*, p. 25). He was co-heir of the barony of Valoines through his mother. In right of his wife (m. about 1270–1, 1292) he had the life-rent of Chilham Castle and the barony. (See further 'Sir Alexander Balliol', by Joseph Bain, in *The Genealogist* (N.S.), iv (1880), 141–3, and *D.N.B.*, s.v. Balliol.) In 1266 the barony was in the custody of Queen Eleanor of Provence, niece of Thomas, Count of Savoy.

6. *The Custody of* MAMINOT. Twenty-four knights. Walkeling Maminot, nephew of William Peverel of Dover, had held Dover for the Empress in 1138. He held 28 fees in 14 Hen. II. His custody passed to Walchelin his son and heir in 3 Ric. I, and then through his sister and co-heir to Geoffrey de Say her husband (d. 1216). Geoffrey answered for 28 fees in 16 John and for 17 fees in ten counties of the fees of Maminot in 8 Hen. III. Another Geoffrey died 1271/2 leaving a son and heir William aged nineteen (*Cal. IPM, Hen. III*, no. 813). This William de Say is no. 2 on the roll.

William had to maintain a certain house in Dover Castle (ibid.) and to maintain part of Rochester bridge. He held also Brougham in Kent by barony. He married a Mandevill heiress.

From this it may be assumed that each custody had its 'house' in Dover Castle.

Nicholas Pesun (no. 45), Bohun of Midhurst (no. 36), and Cudham (nos. 253, 255) all held of William de Say.

7. *Custody of* PORT *of Basing, co. Hants.* Twelve knights. Adam de Port *temp.* Hen. II adopted the name of St. John (Dugdale, *Baronage*, s.v. Port). See no. 91.

8 (and 2). *Custody of* CREVEQUER. Five knights. Robert de Crevequer (no. 3) was the fifth baron (*fl.* 1262 (aged 24)–1288). Ralph of Sandwich (no. 10) seems to have been his heir in 1263. In 1236 a Crevequer paid £100

relief for the lands of William de Abrincis, whose daughter he had married (Dugdale, *Baronage*, p. 592), thus inheriting Custody no. 2.

9. *Custody of* FITZWILLIAM. Six knights. The most obscure but most important in the history of the roll and of the castle, because it points to the origin of castle-guard in the years immediately following the Conquest. This is also suggested by the traditional names of the Custodies, as given by Campbell and used in this list.

There is no trace of a FitzWilliam on the roll, but this is not surprising. Roger FitzWilliam, alias Roger de Breteuil, Earl of Hereford (*fl.* 1071–5), was a younger son of William Fitz Osbern, to whose earldom and English estates he succeeded on his father's death in 1071. He was, says William of Malmesbury, 'a youth of hateful perfidy'. This Fitz William lost his lands as a result of his conspiracy in 1075 with the Earl of Norfolk at 'the Bridale of Norwich'.[1] Thus, if the names of the Custodies mean anything, they must have been established before 1075. Furthermore, when we find that Mr. Hugh Fitz William of Sprotsbrough had in 1563 an ancient copy of the Dering Roll we are prepared to lend some credence to the claim of his family to be descended from a companion (if not a natural son as they claimed) of the Conqueror.[2]

The Hereford tenants on the Dering roll who possibly held FitzWilliam lands are:

81.   Alan Plokenet of Somerset and Dorset.
86.   William and Reginald de Braose of Bramber and Brecon.
162.   Maurice de Berkely.
172.   William de Audley.
175.   Theobald de Verdun (PRA, 34. Hereford retinue on Dunstable roll).
176.   Roger de Clifford of Eardisley.

[1] Ordericus Vitalis, bk. IV, cap. xiii. There is a Thomas le fitz William who bears *masculy d'Ermine et de Goules* as no. 132 on Glover's Roll, this being also the coat of Richard de la Rokele who is no. 131.

[2] See *DNB*, s.v. Sir William Fitz William of Green's Norton (*fl.* 1460 ?–1534), Sheriff of London.

231.   Grimbald Pauncefot (King's knight and M.P. for Here-
       fordshire 1304–5).
266.   Richard de Welles (*IPM*, A.D. 1283).
276.   John Dodingeseles (PRA, 125).
290.   Godfrey de Baskervile of Eardisley (M.P. for Hereford-
       shire 1300, cf. PRA, 151).

The suggestion that they owed castle-guard to Dover as
'FitzWilliam tenants' is quite gratuitous, but no other
reason for their presence on the Roll has been found.

Dover tenants: Castle-guard: on the Dering Roll

No. 44. Stephen de Bacton of Kearnsey owed 5s. castle-guard to
       Dover for a fee to Sir J. de Nortwode (q.v.). *IPM*, no. 605
       (14 Ed. I).
No. 139. William de Bodiham ('Lodiham') of Crek and Bodiham
       in Norfolk owed castle-guard of 1 fee to Dover (*IPM*, *Hen.*
       III, no. 504) for 2 fees, and two parts of a suit at the court of
       Haughley ('Hagenet').
No. 36. John de Bohun of Midhurst (*IPM*, ii. no. 533) held New-
       timber through his wife, of William de Say (no. 2) for ½ a fee.
No. 280. Baldwin de Boliers, *o.s.p.*, 1264 (*Cal. IPM*, *Hen. III*,
       no. 590), tenant of Wm. de Say. Cf. no. 36 above.
Nos. 14, 61. Bertram de Crioil (no. 14) and Nicholas de Sandwich
       (alias de Crioil) (no. 61) shared the 14 fees of the barony of
       Folkestone (= Avranches, Custody 2) (*Rot. Hund.* i. 226),
       and Bertram held 'Estwelle' in Kent by 20s. p.a. for castle-
       guard to Dover, *Cal. IPM*, no. 270 (A.D. 1295), cf. *IPM*,
       Hen. III, no. 774.
No. 77. Gatton, Hamo de, *Cal. IPM, Hen. III*, no. 581 (A.D. 1264).
       Two fees of the barony of Peverel [of Dover] and castle-guard
       to Dover for 2 fees.
Nos. 206, 209. Grey, Nicholas and Bernard. Robert de Grey held
       Ouresby in Lincs. in chief in 1276 and owed castle-guard to
       Dover. It was held from him by Nevile (see nos. 132, 200),
       Rot. Hund. i. 360. See under Arsic.
No. 71. Richard de Hugham, 10s. castle-guard for 1 fee of Chil-
       ham (*Cal. IPM*, 1274, no. 58).
No. 247. Ralph de Jarpenville, 10s. castle-guard to Dover for

manor of Lacenden for 1 fee of Haughley (the Constable's honour). *Cal. IPM*, nos. 423, 472.

No. 72. John of Sandwich was a co-heir of Crevequer (Custody no. 2).

No. 70. Ivon of Shillingheld was a tenant of Chilham.

No. 156. Hugh de Turbervile (*IPM, Hen. III*, nos. 250, 923, shows *Rich.* de T. owing guard to Dover and suit to Haughley).

No. 275. Otho de Grandison occurs probably as a co-heir of Nicholas of Mameins of Kent (no. 112, PRA, 296).

No. 91. John de St. John inherited from Adam de Port of Basing (Custody of Port, no. 7).

[Not on roll] John de Ingoldsthorp held 1 fee in East Raynham and Ilsyngton in Norfolk doing castle-guard at Dover and suit at 'Hasle' (*Cal. IPM, Ed. I*, no. 472).

No. 30. William de Orlenstone held the manor of Orlenstone in Kent in chief, by service of two knights, of the honour of 'Hacenet' (Haughley) and 20s. yearly for the guard of Dover Castle (*Cal. IPM, Ed. I*, no. 527, and *Hen. III*, no. 879).

No. 135. Lucas de Vienne of Osprenge in Kent paid $7\frac{1}{2}d.$ every twenty weeks for castle-guard at Dover (cf. no. 214), i.e. $\frac{1}{16}$ of a fee.

[Not on roll] Ralph de Gatele in 1252 owed 20s. p.a. for castle-guard to Dover, for Gatele in Norfolk (*Cal. IPM, Hen. III*, no. 237. For 2 fees ?).

No. 214. Ralph de Eastling ('Eslingge') held Osprenge manor of the honour of Peverel for $\frac{1}{8}$ fee, suit at Osprenge and 15d. every twenty weeks for castle-guard at Dover (*Cal. IPM*, vol. iii, no. 460). He also held the manor of Eastling of Sir Alexander de Balliol of his manor of Chilham, paying 52s. castle-guard at Dover. (Cf. no. 135.)

Nos. 7, 153. Geoffrey (153) and Robert (7) de Camville are on the Roll. Henry de 'Cramevill' of Reynham in Essex paid £3 p.a. for that manor and three others for guard of Dover Castle and all services (*IPM, Hen. III*, no. 727).

[Not on roll] Emery Batayl held in chief in 'Lacedone' and Broadwell in Essex by service of one fee and 10s. castle-guard to Dover and suit to Haughley. Of this he sold to two persons twelve acres 'on which they built many fair houses'— a medieval housing estate? *Cal. IPM, Hen. III*, no. 250 (A.D. 1253), p. 63.

Note that the commutation rate is 10*s*. on the fee for nos. 30, 135, 214 and Emery Batyl (*above*).

Of the Constables Richard de Grey of Codnor (no. 209), Bertram de Crioil (no. 14), and Penchester (no. 6) are mentioned.

V

ST. GEORGE'S ROLL[1]

ST. George's roll is closely associated with the Welsh marches, and, as will be seen, was probably drawn up for Roger Mortimer II (1237/8–October 1282) or one of his family. Apart from the Welsh and the Scots and Amaury de Montfort, there are no foreign or outlandish coats.

Roger Mortimer was half Welsh, and this is surely the key to the roll. He was the eldest son of Ralph Mortimer and Gwladys Ddu (Gladys the Black), daughter of Llewelyn ap Jorwerth. His contemporary Welsh and English relatives appear on the roll. He ruled his estates from 1247, paying 2,000 marks to avoid escheat and wardship. In 1253 he was knighted by Henry III in person.[2] From his wife Matilda de Braose he received a third of Brecon as his share of the great Marshal inheritance in south Wales, England, and Ireland.

Mortimer came to the front at once in 1258. He was one of the Baronial committees of Twelve, Fifteen, and Twenty-four, but from the end of 1261 he was always a

---

[1] St. George's roll *olim* Charles' roll, 'E' to Papworth, is printed in *Archaeologia*, vol. 39 (1864), 'Three Rolls of Arms of the Latter Part of the Thirteenth Century', by W. S. Walford and C. S. Percival, as the third of three rolls, the others being the 'Society of Antiquaries' Roll 17', now styled Charles' roll ('F' to Papworth), a fifteenth-century facsimile copy, and Walford's roll. See *CEMRA*, pp. 19–24, where all are dated *c.* 1285, for a full description.

Walford's Roll is a blazoned roll of 180/5 names, many of them foreign, of kings, dukes, counts, and knights. It exists in copies of two versions, one made in 1607 by Nicholas Charles, Lancaster, in Harl. MS. 6589, fol. 12–12ᵇ; the other edited by Thomas Hearne from John Leland's *Collectanea*, first ed., London, 1715, vol. i, pp. 897–905. On the foreign coats in Walford's roll see Max Prinet in *Moyen Age*, 2ᵉ sér., t. XXV (1923), pp. 223–56.

[2] *Ann. Theok.* (RS), i. 152.

royalist. Sir Maurice Powicke says of him, 'Roger Mortimer more than any other man broke the fortunes of Earl Simon, and by rallying the Marchers, sustained Edward's independence as heir to the throne, and afterwards as king.'[1] For it was his provision of a fast horse that enabled Edward to elude his captors in May 1265.[2] After the royalist victory at Evesham in August, and the surrender of Kenilworth castle next year, he received the custody of Hereford castle with the county. His liberty of Cleobury Mortimer in Shropshire was made autonomous.[3]

In 1270 Mortimer, Walter Giffard, Richard of Cornwall, and two others were appointed guardians of Edward's children, lands, and interests in England for the duration of Edward's crusade. Mortimer, Giffard, and Richard of Cornwall became automatically a Regency in November 1272 on the death of Henry III. Though not an earl, Mortimer could thus regard himself as the leading banneret in the kingdom. The Round Table that he held at Kenilworth in 1279 was attended by a hundred knights and as many ladies, and was intended to celebrate his retirement after twenty-six years of strenuous knighthood. Like Gloucester, with whom he quarrelled in 1267, Mortimer was a man of violent temper, after Edward's own heart. He was richly rewarded in lands for his services, and it is perhaps a recognition of his great position that in St. George's roll he comes next after the earls and the King of Scotland.

In 1281, probably in October, Mortimer concluded with his kinsman Llewelyn a 'treaty of peace and indivisible concord',[4] by which both parties bound themselves, subject to their respective fealties to the King of England, to stand together with all their strength against all mortal men, both in time of war and peace, on pain of excommunication. The roll of arms was probably drawn up

[1] F. M. Powicke, *The Thirteenth Century*, p. 404.
[2] *Flores*, iii. 2.   [3] Eyton, *Shropshire*, iii. 40; iv. 221–2.
[4] J. G. Edwards, *Littere Wallie* (1940), p. lxii, and no. 194.

between the tournament at Kenilworth in 1279 and this agreement of 1281. Perhaps, like Collins' Roll, it was meant to symbolize the birth of a new era of international amity, not only the culmination of his own career, but the pacification of Wales, the marriage of Llewelyn ap Grufydd with Eleanor de Montfort, Amaury's sister, at Worcester on 13 October 1278. So Amaury is here too, and on no other English roll of arms, together with five of the Mortimers and four of his Welsh relatives.[1] It was in all probability made, as a painted roll, before the dream of peaceful co-operation with Llewelyn and the Welsh had vanished, and the climate of Anglo-Welsh relations was drastically changed.[2]

The general rolls of arms were living things, like family trees and some chronicles. They grew by accretion, particularly perhaps if they were borrowed, or alienated through the death of the owner. St. George's Roll, beginning as a regional roll, contains many knights of the shire, and sheriffs of the next generation, men who held office between 1295 and 1307, and many knights whose homes were far away from Wigmore. The roll, with its 677 names, is far too long to be referred in its present form to any one centre.[3] So many knights never coexisted in any one march. Like the Society of Antiquaries' roll and perhaps Collins' Roll, it has become amorphous. It is a matter for speculation whether the compilers included every knight who chanced to venture in arms within his

---

[1] Neither here nor on Charles' Roll do we find Edmund Mortimer, already an active soldier who succeeded his father Roger II in 1282. The relation with Charles' Roll is very close and both probably derived from a painted thirteenth-century original. They have 300 names in common, as is apparent from the collation made in *Arch.* xxxix.

[2] Compare the 'false dawn' in Anglo-Scottish relations at the Parliament of Berwick in 1296, thought to be reflected in Collins' Roll.

[3] St. George's Roll begins, as was the fashion, with a few dead earls (e.g. Chester d. 1232, Salisbury, Aumale d. 1260, followed by the King of Scotland and two attendant earls, Atholl and Angus) and then puts Roger Mortimer. It contains men who died in 1226 and many who were dead by 1254. The blazon is not contemporary.

province, or possibly without pressing the evidence too far one might write Province.

St. George's Roll provides the earliest clue to what must have been a common phenomenon in the thirteenth century, the seignorial herald. For it is to be remembered that not one tournament in a hundred was a Royal Tournament and in Edward I's time we can only name the 'little battle' of Chalon and the tournament at Nefyn. The royal heralds were busy prohibiting tournaments, not organizing them. But for the organization of baronial jousts and Round Tables, the presence of heralds was equally necessary, and it is hardly to be supposed that the men whom the king sent down to prohibit them changed their tabards and operated on behalf of the contestants. Happily it is not necessary to postulate the existence of heralds in private service. It can be proved. The relationship between them and the royal heralds is quite unknown, but it can be shown that, like other seignorial officials, they could regard service with a magnate as a stepping-stone to service at court. We may postulate a herald for every march, whose province is simply the extent of his lord's power and influence. The herald of the Scottish March comes to light at Falkirk,[1] as 'le Rey Marchis', but the Mortimer herald is not known by name until 1337, when Edmund Mortimer, Earl of the March, created John O'thelake his herald by the name of March.[2] He followed the usual careerist pattern, as Walter le Rey had done eighty years earlier, by becoming on Edmund Mortimer's death in 1381 'J. March unus heraldorum rex ad arma, Rex Norreys'.

A note may be useful on Welsh gentlemen of coat armour in the period 1278–c. 1310.

The list of 'Swan Knights' contains Griffin filius Griffin de la Pole (no. 157), Morgan ap Mereduc (no. 97), Hugh Howel (no. 109.)[3]

---

[1] *Infra*, pp. 103 ff.   [2] Wagner, *Heralds and Heraldry*, p. 36.

[3] I have numbered them according to the order of their occurrence in Ashmole's list. The coats are not given.

The earliest painted shield noticed is in Penarth MS. 28, p. 46, in the Welsh National Library at Aberystwyth. The manuscript is catalogued as 'last quarter of the twelfth century' but is really a manuscript of *c.* 1240, written in a neat court hand, containing the Laws of Howel Dda. The shield, crudely sketched, seems to be Per pale *Or* and *Arg.* with a Canton *Vert* in dexter chief.[1]

Welsh Gentlemen of Coat Armour

On St. George's Roll the following Welsh coats occur:

No. 7. Llewelyn or William ap Griffith: Quarterly de *Gu.* & *Or* en les quartiers leopards passans de contre couleur.

No. 26. ? David: Quarterly *Or* & *Az.* with four leopards de contre couleur.

No. 27. 'Blothow': *Or* ung sautour *Gu.* iv rondels *Gu.*

No. 75. Griffith ap Wenwynwyn: D'*Or* a lion rampant *Gu.* His daughter married Fulk FitzWarin (*Cal. Cl. R.*, 1277, p. 374).

No. 78. Robert Howell: *Sa.* a cross *Or* = Antiq. 59. Philip ap Howel appointed Constable of Builth for five years in 1279 (*Cal. Fine Rolls*, p. 423).

No. 151 [de la Pole]: *Or* a lion rampant *Gu.* a border engrailed *Sa.*

No. 183. Howell ap Meryk: Paly d'*Or* & *Az.* & i fess *Gu.* in which are iii mullets *Arg.* Cf. Hoel son of Maurice at Builth (*Cal. Cl. R.*, Apr. 1279, 527).

No. 280. Ede' de Hovel: Quarterly de *Gu.* & *Arg.* indented.

No. 656: Howel Ap Res [Rhys] de *Gu.* & chevron and three pierced stars *Arg.*

The seven Mortimer coats are nos. 22 (Roger), 24 (Roger), each with the Mortimer inescucheon, argent or ermine, 38 (William), 40 (Geoffrey), 65 (John), 78 (Robert of Richard's Castle, d. 1287?), 545 (William).

Any 'de la Pole' occurring in the earlier portion of St. George's Roll is obviously Pole of Welshpool, from the context. Hence no. 151 above enables us to refer PRA 1051, Le sire de la Pole, *de Or a un lion de goules* among the *abatues*, to Owen de la Pole the castellan of

---

[1] It must be borne in mind that *Or* and *Arg.*, and *Azure* and *Vert*, are liable to confusion through the deterioration of the tinctures. The coat might belong to the same family as that of 'Howel ap Mered'' (St. George's Roll, no. 183).

Welshpool, co. Montgomery, who was a *Commilito* in 1285 and King's banneret in 1286, 1290. He (or a grandson) is Collins no. 476, *Or* a lion rampant *Gu.* a label of 5 points *Az.* For the minority of Griffin de la Pole (late *Owen* de la Pole) see *Cal. Fine Rolls* (A.D. 1295), pp. 354, 358. *G. filius G.* [*for* O.?] *de la Pole* was a Swan Knight in 1306 (Ashmole, no. 57). Lowys de la Pole, *de Or a un lion de Goulis e un baston de Sable*, is PRA 950 (Cheshire), cf. Collins 478. An unfinished coat in Collins 592 is *Or* a chief . . . for Philip de la Pole.

Sir William de la Pole, of Ravenser Odd and Hull (knight in 1296, d. 1329), who married the daughter of John Rotenheryng and was grandfather of Michael de la Pole, first Earl of Suffolk, is not here in question, as he is not found on the rolls of arms used in this book.

VI

SIR ROBERT CLIFFORD AND THE ROLLS

(1) CLIFFORD AND COLLINS' ROLL

T H E Welsh have always in chronicle and record been passionately devoted to genealogies, often showing descent from Brutus. This facet of the national character sometimes emerges in the form of a jactatory list of famous persons or heroic ancestors, as in biblical genealogies, and in no way detracts from the value of the Marcher rolls as a record of fact contemporary with the compiler. This became a feature of a number of the rolls not connected with Wales. The rolls associated with the Scottish border do not include mythical persons, though they may, like Collins' Roll, cover two generations,[1] either retrospectively or by accretion.

Collins is a general roll of 598 (Erdeswicke's version) or 720 (Dethick's version) names, extant in sixteenth- and seventeenth-century copies of a thirteenth-century painted original.[2] Version I, which has been the one used in this book, begins with *Roy de England*, *Le Prince*, but *Le Prince* is not in Version II and the occurrence of this style is not found before 1306 when the Prince was knighted. He was given Wales indeed in 1301, but in the *Song of Caerlaverock* it is his father who is Prince of Wales—by right of conquest. But we do not know the date of the blazon.

The list of earls presents some points of interest. The inclusion of an Earl of Chester may point to the origin of the claims of Bruce, Balliol, and Hastings to that earldom,

---

[1] e.g. John and Philip Marmiun (nos. 135, 169); William and Robert Mortain (nos. 113, 539), each pair being assigned the same arms.
[2] *CEMRA*, pp. 24–25.

which they had maintained long after the death in 1237 of Ranulph le Scot, the last Norman earl. Robert Bruce, son of the claimant, was at that time in Edward's favour.[1] Secondly, the Earl of Lincoln was in Gascony at the time. The Earl of Lancaster had sailed thither from Plymouth in November 1295 with his nineteen bannerets, and on his death in June 1296 was succeeded by Lincoln who 'held on, almost deserted, until the truce of 9 October 1297'.[2] But a painted roll was a work of art, and, though the occasion at Berwick was probably taken advantage of to compile this roll, it is not strictly an 'occasional roll'. It is indeed reminiscent, in either version, of the young man of Japan who wrote verses that no one could scan because, as he said, 'I put everything into the last line that I possibly can'. It was better to include a man who might have been there than to risk offending a potential patron. Thus a list of earls in such rolls is merely what in formal Latin composition would be called (at that date) the *benivolentie captatio*, or, in a speech, the *Arenga*. This feature is much less marked in Collins than in some other rolls.

This roll is as clearly a product of the Scottish border as St. George's Roll is of the Marches of Wales. There are a number of Scottish earls and knights, highland and lowland, also—a crucial instance—the Earl of Ulster and some Irish followers.[3] But there is no King of Scotland.

---

[1] Father and son were both active on Edward's side in 1296. The young man who became king succeeded to the earldom of Carrick in his father's lifetime (Barron, *Scottish War of Independence*, 2nd ed., p. 126).

[2] F. M. Powicke, *The Thirteenth Century*, p. 649.

[3] The Irish arrived at Stirling, where Edward I was 14–20 June 1296, before Balliol's abdication in July. The battle of Dunbar had already been fought on 28 April and the Scots routed by Warenne with huge slaughter (Powicke, *The Thirteenth Century*, pp. 614–15). The Irish contingents was led by Richard de Burgh, Earl of Ulster. The names of the leaders and the size of their retinues, to a total of 310 heavy, 266 light cavalry, and 2,576 foot, are in Stevenson, *Documents*, ii. 124. John Wogan, the Justiciar of Ireland, was there (no. 180), and six members of the Botiler family (including Theobald le Botiler (no. 117)), Maurice de Rocheford (cf. no. 204, Rauf de R.), Hugh Purcel and Eustace Poer (not on the roll), and John Fitz Thomas (cf. no. 203, William). The Irish barons had been summoned by writ of 1 March 1296 (*Parl. Writs*, i. 275–7).

These facts alone are sufficient to stamp the roll as coming from the North. Each of Edward I's professional captains, or their heralds, would have some such roll, though not necessarily one that ran to such a length.

There is little doubt that Collins' Roll was compiled *c*. 1295–6,[1] and so the position of Roger Clifford (no. 23) immediately after the earls is puzzling. Roger had married a Vipont co-heiress, but their son Robert had no footing in the March until he took seisin in 1295. If 'Roger' and not 'Robert' is really intended this entry is somewhat incongruous. It is just possible that the meteoric rise of Sir Robert Clifford had attracted a retrospective glory to his father's name. The textual history of the roll makes speculation unprofitable, but Sir Robert Clifford is, as will appear, important in the heraldic history of his times and the year 1296 saw the beginning of his distinguished military career.

There was no Roger Clifford in 1296. The younger Roger (father of Robert) predeceased his father in Wales in 1282 and Robert's grandfather, the elder Roger, survived till 1286. What happened to young Robert is not known, but his father's marriage caused the migration of the Clifford family seat from Clifford Castle in South Wales to Appleby in Westmorland. Robert was born about Easter 1273 and is likely to have remained with his mother until he was seven. Whether, following the custom of the age Robert then became a page in another noble household, and whether his mother remained in south Wales or returned to Westmorland, is not known. There is only one Clifford on the roll, and whichever Roger is meant, he had been dead at least ten years, and furthermore had no claim to such a prominent place upon the roll except in right of his wife or daughter-in-law as the case might be. It seems possible that young Robert is really intended, for he made his name in action not long after he had taken seisin

[1] e.g. Simon Fraser bears a label (colour unspecified) of three points in Collins (no. 387), but none in Falkirk (no. 79) or Caerlaverock (no. 54).

of his share of the Vipont inheritance in 1295. The compiler of the roll may be excused for ignoring him or mistaking his name.[1]

Thus Robert inherited from his grandfather, when he was about 13 years old,[2] being 22 or 23 at the Battle of Dunbar in 1296. From his mother he inherited half the shrievalty of Westmorland,[3] and became the *Castellanus de Appleby*, the title accorded to him in the Barons' letter to the Pope of 1300.

Clifford's active career began shortly after 4 March 1296,[4] when he was appointed as one of two 'Captains and Wardens of our peace for the defence of Cumberland'. In pursuance of this, by indenture dated 2 April 1296 at Berwick,[5] shortly before the battle of Dunbar (28 April), he agreed to provide 140 men-at-arms (i.e. cavalry) and

[1] The pedigree is thus, as in G.E.C.:

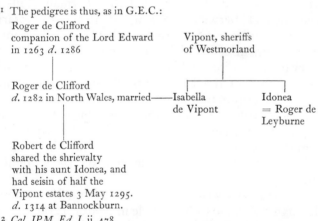

Roger de Clifford
companion of the Lord Edward
in 1263 *d.* 1286

Vipont, sheriffs
of Westmorland

Roger de Clifford
d. 1282 in North Wales, married——Isabella
de Vipont

Idonea
= Roger de
Leyburne

Robert de Clifford
shared the shrievalty
with his aunt Idonea, and
had seisin of half the
Vipont estates 3 May 1295.
d. 1314 at Bannockburn.

[2] *Cal. IPM. Ed. I*, ii. 478.

[3] The partition of the Vipont shrievalty led to a dispute which had been settled by 1283 (*IPM*, loc. cit.). See also W. A. Morris, *The Medieval English Sheriff to 1300* (Manchester, 1927), pp. 179–80, where it is incorrectly stated that John Fitz-John, the well known baronial leader, was 'presumably his [i.e. Robert de Vipont II's] brother'. Fitz-John was one of Simon de Montfort's importations as sheriff in May 1264.

[4] *Parl. Writs*, i. 278. The commission is said by Miss Reid (*EHR*, xxxii (1917)) to be identical with that of 7 November 1295 for the custody and defence of the sea shore in Kent and Sussex (*Parl. Writs*, i. 271).

[5] Stevenson, *Documents*, ii. 36–37 (= Bain, *Cal. Docs. Scot.* ii. 170).

500 foot, for which he would take a fixed sum, as for his own household, to defend the march of Scotland until three weeks after Easter (i.e. until 16 April). During this period he was to do his utmost to take hostages of the forest of Selkirk, the moor of Cavers, Liddisdale, Eskdale, Ennisdale, Annandale, Moffatsdale, and Galloway, and the other lands which have come to the power of the king. He was to receive the arrears of the £800 which the king owed him, for his residence in Scotland and the March from Saturday next after St. Hilary until 2 April 1296, and to be repaid within eight days for the loss of any horses.

Clifford's contract ran out on 16 April and he is lost to view until 4 June 1297,[1] a gap of fifteen months including the Battle of Dunbar on 28 April 1296.

About this time was compiled the Ragman Roll[2] of proceedings at Berwick (28 August 1296)—a notarial record of homages and fealties at what is usually known as the Parliament of Berwick.[3] This was a gathering of the chivalry of two nations held on the conclusion of Edward's triumphal tour of the Highlands, during which he had ravished the Coronation Stone from Scone. The Ragman Roll is noticed here because the seals attached to it have prompted its description by Sir William Ramsay as 'the ur-armorial of the Scottish gentry'.[4] The king was at Berwick for over three weeks, leaving on 16 September 1296.

There had been writs of summons to 200 English and Irish tenants to come to Newcastle in March 1296 'to seek a remedy against Balliol for his infringement of his sworn obligation', but our roll of arms is not related to the

---

[1] *Infra*, pp. 112 f.

[2] Bain, *Cal. Docs. Scot.* ii. 189–92 (no. 823), edited in 1834 for the Bannatyne Club by T. Thomas.

[3] The meeting was officially described as a parliament of the magnates of both realms (Bain, ii. 196), though the title of parliament is denied to it by some modern writers.

[4] Ramsay, *Dawn of the Constitution* (1908), p. 433.

muster roll.[1] Collins' roll in its original form was drawn up between 25 August and 15 September 1296, because it includes the Irish but excludes Balliol. The roll also includes[2] prisoners who were sent to English castles (Atholl, Menteith, Ross, the younger John Comyn of Badenoch, Richard Siward, and William Sinclair, as well as many who submitted and made their peace). Ten thousand and fifty-two are said to have been slain in the battle,[3] but bearing in mind the aptitude of calculators at that date to slip from '99' to '1000' if using the unfamiliar Arabic numerals,[4] it will be easy for sceptical persons to lop off a nought.

One copy of the roll may then have been made for William de Beauchamp, the Earl of Warwick who died shortly after Dunbar, but far more probably for his son Guy, a young banneret at the time. This is suggested by what is known of Guy's personal tastes, and by the later history of the roll, which in the fifteenth century was interpolated in the Yorkist interest,[5] and owned by Warwick the King-maker.

Guy of Warwick is the third of the barons to migrate to the north. The change in the centre of gravity of political and military interest in the late thirteenth and early fourteenth centuries is exemplified by Clifford's move from Clifford Castle in south Wales to Appleby in Westmorland,

---

[1] The writ of summons is dated 16 December 1295 (*Parl. Writs*, i. 275-7).

[2] Richard of Cornwall or Almain, son of the King of the Romans, is on the roll. He was killed at Berwick before the battle (Ramsay, p. 426). The roll is an authority for his coat of arms: *Argent* on a fess (?) 3 plates *Or* (no. 266).

[3] Barth. Cott., pp. 310-12; Hem., old ed., pp. 95-96; *Flores*, pp. 97-98.

[4] See the Introduction to my edition of Richard de Bury's *Liber Epistolaris* (Roxburghe Club, 1950).

[5] Beauchamp, Nevile, and Woodville additions were made before about 1400 (*CEMRA*, pp. 26-27), in the time of Warwick the King-maker's father, i.e. the King-maker did not possess it as Constable of England, but because he was a Beauchamp, and had inherited it ultimately perhaps from Guy. Clifford and Guy were closely associated in the later years of their lives (e.g. at the Dunstable tournament and in the matter of the administration of Clifford's property in 1314-15).

by Henry Percy, 'founder' of his line, who moved from Hampshire to Alnwick in 1308, and by Warwick, who bought Castle Barnard from the Crown in 1307.

Warwick (b. 1271 × 5, succ. 1298, died 1315) was a banneret in Flanders in August 1297, with a retinue of two knights and eleven esquires. Returning thence with the king he fought at Falkirk, and is no. 24 on the Caerlaverock Roll,[1] where he is oddly described as a *very good neighbour*. He attended Edward I's death 7 July 1307, when he was warned by him against Gaveston.[2] This warning he took to heart, and alone of the earls refused to be reconciled with Gaveston in 1309.[3] Gaveston would hardly have endorsed this testimonial to the man he nicknamed the 'Black Dog of Arden'. This judgement and its endorsement by Professor Tout, who spoke of Warwick as a 'cultivated aristocratic ruffian of the Renascence',[4] does not accord with the verdict of contemporary chroniclers[5] to whom Tout never allowed sufficient weight. As a marcher lord and hereditary sheriff of Worcestershire, Guy had an influence out of all proportion to his Warwick castle estate. He had the staff, the feodaries, and all the machinery of a shire as well as the resources of an earldom, combined with martial tastes, if he wanted a roll of arms.

[1] Warwick bore 'a red banner with a fess of gold and crusilly' (cf. PRA, no. 10). [2] *DNB*, s.v. Guy de Beauchamp, art. by J. H. R.

[3] *Chron. Ed. I & II*, ii. 160.

[4] T. F. Tout, *The Place of Edward II in English History* (2nd ed., p. 154).

[5] 'Virum sapientem et probum' (Lanercost, p. 216); 'Homo discretus et bene literatus, per quem totum regnum Anglie sapientia prefulgebat' (*Ann. Lond.*, p. 236). According to Trokelowe (pp. 72–73) the Earl of Lincoln had a high opinion of him. The *Vita Edwardi Secundi* (ed. N. Denholm-Young), p. 63, says convincingly: 'In 1315 if the Earl of Warwick had been alive the whole country would have been behind him. By his advice and skill the Ordinances were framed . . . in wisdom and counsel he had no peer.' He says this in spite of Guy's behaviour as Gaveston's executioner. But it would be unfair to read back into his whole career this one discreditable episode. By his will made on Holy Rood day 25 Ed. I (14 Sept. 1297) he was to be buried with the Franciscans at Worcester, if possible. His two 'great horses' were to carry his armour at his funeral, for the solemnizing of which he gave £200, and left £100 to maintain two knights in the Holy Land (Dugdale, *Bar.* i. 229).

(II) FALKIRK ROLL

One of the heroes of the Falkirk Roll is Henry de Percy (1273–1314) who in 1308 bought Alnwick from Anthony Bek, so that the Percies moved their northern home from Topcliffe on the Swale near Ripon to the Scottish border. The main line of the Percies continued at Alnwick until 1670. This Henry de Percy, who bore *Or* a lion rampant *Az*, is described in the chronicle of Alnwick as pre-eminent for his skill in tournaments and more famous and powerful than any of his predecessors. He was in fact, says Kingsford,[1] 'the virtual founder of his house'. The Percies were a Lancashire and Yorkshire family with large interests in Hampshire, through the marriage of William de Percy with Emma, daughter of Hugh de Port; and Sussex, through the marriage of Agnes de Percy with Jocelin, brother of Henry I's second wife Adelaide, which brought to the Percy family the great estate of Petworth in Sussex. Jocelin's brother Ralph (*c.* 1170–1244) was an active supporter of Louis of France against King John—hence the presence of members of the family on the Dering Roll (q.v.).

This Sir Henry de Percy, or, if we are writing with an eye on the fourteenth century, Lord Percy, stands at present as the first private person in England whose herald is known. Himself a famous man in his day, it is not surprising to find that he had an equally famous King of Arms in his following at the battle of Falkirk. Percy was of full age in Gascony in 1294 and in March 1296 went with the king to Scotland. He was knighted before Berwick and was present at the Battle of Dunbar. On 8 September 1296 he was made Warden of Galloway,[2] and from

---

[1] Art. Percy in *DNB* by C. L. Kingsford, citing De Fonblanque, *Annals of the House of Percy*, ii. 50–71. As this is a rare book it may save some scholar's time if I mention that it adds nothing to our knowledge of the Percies in the thirteenth century.

[2] Stevenson, *Docs.* ii. 100, 110,

his headquarters at Carlisle may have been with Clifford in an incursion into Annandale.[1]

If I understand C. L. Kingsford aright,[2] he thought that Lord Percy 'missed' the Battle of Falkirk—an error which has since taken root—and Dr. Morris in his Appendix on the Numbers at Falkirk did not notice until too late that Henry Percy with four of the earls had made a special contract with the king for the expedition. Because of this contract, printed by Henry Gough[3] in his able but neglected edition of the Falkirk Roll of Arms together with the horse-inventories and many other documents relating to the campaign, Percy and the said earls, though in the Roll of Arms, are not in the inventories. Hence the Earl of Arundel and William le Latimer, too, are missed. Dr. Morris (p. 290) allows the earl 4 lances, but the joint contract of the Earl and Latimer shows a total of 27 knights and 110 troopers. In this way Dr. Morris and all subsequent writers have omitted about a quarter or even a third of the heavy cavalry—through neglecting to correlate the Roll of Bannerets with the horse-inventories. If a man had made a contract he did not register his horses: if he served *ad vadia* he did, because he was entitled to *restauracio equorum*. In all the campaigns of Edward I the qoint is of some importance if a just estimate of numbers is to be obtained.

Percy was with his uncle Warenne, in the fourth squadron, with his blue lion on a gold shield. In December 1298 he received £769. 3s. 4d. for three months' service with 50 barbed horses, i.e. the 50 he had contracted for.[4]

---

[1] Ibid. ii. 170–3, 186; Hem. (old ed., ii. 146–7). The force is said to have consisted of 100 cavalry and 10,000 (!) foot. It was based on Carlisle and returned on Christmas Eve. The raid was repeated in Lent 1298.

[2] *DNB*, s.v. Percy.

[3] H. Gough, *Scotland in 1298* (Edinburgh, 1888). The contract made by the Earls of Surrey (for 100 men-at-arms), Norfolk (150), Hereford (90), Gloucester (100), Warwick (30), and Percy (50), which is summarized in Appendix only by Morris (p. 285), is printed *in extenso* by Gough, pp. 64–65, apparently from KRMR, m. 106.

[4] Bain, ii. 1044.

He next appears with his grandfather at the siege of
Caerlaverock in July 1300.

In respect of our knowledge of the retinues employed
Falkirk is unique for a thirteenth-century battle.[1] It is also
outstanding in the history of the Heralds. For Percy had
with him in his retinue a Herald King of Arms, Walter le
Rey Marchis, who exemplifies in his career the clerical
and knightly practice of taking service with a private lord
before seeking a wider field for ambition in the royal household. Unless we count the old Marshal's entourage at the
beginning of the century, Walter is the first known herald
in private service in England. In view of his known prominence in his profession it is tempting to suggest that
he made the Falkirk Roll for his master, Lord Percy,
in whose March the battle was fought. Other leaders
may have had their own heralds—though this is unlikely
unless they were accustomed to exercise a 'federal'
power—but the making of a roll could well have been
entrusted initially to the herald of the March alone.
The importance of heralds in this period might in a small
way be compared to the evolution of Parliament: it was so
much a part of the general scene that it passed without
comment. Hemingburgh and Nicholas Trivet are the
only two English chroniclers who explicitly mention
heralds in Edward I's lifetime.

Being on Crusade was in itself a recognized excuse for
not attending to legal business, but while serving with the
armed forces of the Crown on other occasions a man

[1] The retinues of some of the 43 bannerets in the King's brigade can be made
up from the horse-inventories and the lists of 'protections' for the expedition.
These are printed by H. Gough, *Scotland in 1298* (1888), side by side with both
versions of the Falkirk Roll of Arms and numerous subsidiary documents. The
careers of many of Edward's knights could be traced from their earlier employment as esquires (*valletti*) in these documents, e.g. Nicholas Vipont, a *valet* at
Falkirk (Gough 198), is a banneret twelve years or so later (PRA, 121). I cannot
find that any writer on heraldry or history has made use of this invaluable book,
from 1888 to the present day, though it is mentioned in Gross's *Bibliography*
(no. 2151). For the textual history of the Falkirk Roll see Wagner, *CEMRA*,
pp. 27–29.

needed special 'letters of protection' and sometimes, like Ralph de Monthermer, Earl Warenne, and Henry Percy, letters of Respite for Crown Debts as well. They also had letters of protection for those going with them, and this is how we come to hear of Walter le Rey, as Percy's herald.

The Falkirk campaign saw the call-up of vast numbers of infantry, about 7,000 of whom were paid for the march from Wales to Scotland and back without seeing any fighting.[1] It was the news of the English defeat at Stirling Bridge (10 September 1297) and the extraction of the *Confirmatio Cartarum* by Bigod and Bohun from the Regency in London that persuaded Edward to make the truce of Vyves-St. Bavon with the French (31 January 1298) and hurry home from Flanders. Landing at Sandwich on 14 March he held a *colloquium speciale* at York on 25 May, and the army was marshalled at Roxburgh at the end of June.[2] When Edward left York he moved towards Edinburgh to co-operate with the North Sea fleet. The Scots were six leagues away at Falkirk. Edward, camping on the moor near Linlithgow, was trampled on by his horse during the night, but rode off next day at dawn, after hearing Mass.[3] The Welsh and south-country infantry had come up via Chester, but they threatened to riot on the field of battle. Wallace's army was on rising ground with a marsh in front. His four circular bodies of troops, with groups of archers in between them, were defended along the whole front by a palisade of roped stakes. The Scots were weak in cavalry, so the Earl Marshal, Hereford, Lincoln (that is, the first brigade) and Anthony Bek (leading the second brigade) attacked the two wings of their position and their cavalry fled. The

---

[1] 3,000 foot were to be levied from Lancashire to serve with R. de Clifford (*CPR*, 14 Nov. 1297, p. 315).

[2] F. M. Powicke, *The Thirteenth Century*, pp. 688 f.

[3] Edward is said to have broken two ribs (Trevet, p. 372; Hem., pp. 179–80; Barth. Cott., pp. 343–4). Hemingburgh states that there were 23, 23, 40, and 25 bannerets respectively in the 'battles'. He identifies the vanguard, the king's battle, and the rearguard. The total agrees precisely with the roll.

pikemen dispersed and the infantry, as at Dunbar, were massacred with enormous loss.

If we exclude the siege of Caerlaverock and Stirling, the Battle of Falkirk provides our only thirteenth-century battle Roll of Arms, i.e. a roll of the bannerets who took part. From the fact that they numbered 111 it could be deduced that there were about 600 knights bachelor, and 900 esquires or *valletti*, for this 6 : 1 ratio is commonly found in cavalry forces of the period. If we accept the totals arrived at by Dr. Morris and accepted by Sir Maurice Powicke[1] there were also some 800 troopers or sergeants, i.e. a total of some 2,300 horsemen. The third brigade included the king, his nephews the two young sons of Edmund of Lancaster, and John of Brittany; also his pensioner John of Bar, the Earl of Warwick, and some Gascons. The fourth brigade was held in reserve with the Earls of Gloucester, Arundel, Oxford, and Pembroke. But it was Edward's brigade (the third) that most effectively took the Scots in the rear of the hedge. The only important English casualties were Sir Brian Jay, the Master of the Templars, and Sir Adam de Welles, a household knight. Wallace fled to France but was handed over and hanged.

The names of the 'simple knights' and esquires that can be recovered are thus almost exclusively those in the royal brigade, the household at war. The esquires—the *valletti* of these rolls—will many of them be knights by the end of the period, and the careers of some hundreds of them could be followed from this time, with the aid of local histories, though with great labour.[2] The horsemen

[1] Powicke, *The Thirteenth Century*, pp. 689–90. Robert Bruce, father of King Robert, was probably fighting for the last time on the English side. His brother Bernard was in the English army (Gough, pp. x, xi). Among the Scots who died were Sir John Stewart of Bonkill, brother of the Steward, Sir John Graham Wallace's 'Right-Hand', one of the MacDuffs of Fife, and Adam Brown.

[2] The roll, which in 1888 was PRO K.R. Army 26 Edw. I $\frac{22}{20}$, is headed *Rotulus de equis Banerettorum, Militum Simplicum, Scutiferorum, Vallettorum Hospicii Regis etc.* The type of entry is *Dominus A.* [who may be clerk or banneret], *Dominus B. miles suus . . ., G.* [etc.] *vallettus suus . . . .*

of the household, the clerks, and the baggage train or Karavan are also included. Mr. John Walwyn, later to become Treasurer of England, was at that time in the retinue of Sir Robert de Tony, the Swan Knight, who had been promoted banneret in November 1297 in Flanders. Walwayn too had been with him since at least 1298.[1]

The roll has descended in two versions, both of them blazoned, not painted rolls, so that if the copies are verbally accurate, it is important that one (the Harl. MS. 6589) says 'Garenne' like the PRA, where the Wrest Park version has Warenne. Other slight differences in the terms of blazon may point in the same direction, and a material addition of certain names of bannerets at the end shows that these two rolls are not copies of the same original but versions made, it is suggested, independently from a muster-roll or pay-roll of some kind. The suggestion is that the Harl. MS. is a copy of a roll made by Lord Percy's herald Wauter le Rey Marchis who was in Percy's retinue at the battle (Percy is no. 99 on the roll) in the fourth brigade with Earl Warenne's reserve.[2] The other version, using the archaic *Wa* for *Ga*, might have descended, as did the owner of the Wrest Park MS. itself,[3] from Reginald de Grey, who is no. 61 upon the roll, in the King's brigade.

Now Grey, baron of Wilton and lord of Ruthin (succ. 1265, d. 1308), had been justiciar of Chester and has been described as 'the young Prince's mentor' in 1297,[4] when he

---

[1] Gough, p. 198, and *EHR* (April 1956), 'The Authorship of the *Vita Edwardi Secundi*', p. 202, by the present author.

[2] For Walter le Rey see also p. 59. He was an important royal herald by 1300.

[3] *Hist. MSS. Comm. Rep.* ii. 6. The blazon of the Harl. MS., as printed by Gough, seems to me to be manifestly superior. The Right Hon. Anne Florence, Dowager Countess Cowper, was heiress of Grey of Ruthin, cr. Earl of Kent 1465. On the other hand the Wrest Park version was brought back from France in the seventeenth century, but the blazon is not French—contrast the Caerlaverock Roll.

[4] He received a barony for services rendered in 1282/3—the barony of Duffryn Clwyd. Ramsay (*Dawn*, p. 448) praises him for his judicial handling of the crisis of 1297.

was Regent of England. It is safe to assume that he, like Percy, would have a herald, and quite possible that his descendant at Wrest Park had inherited her copy of the Falkirk Roll as a family treasure, i.e. the one using the old-fashioned Anglo-Norman spelling.

Note on the Falkirk infantry

There was a growing use of infantry in the thirteenth century. The *jurati ad arma* was the term used in the writs to describe the national militia, the successors under the Assize of Arms (A.D. 1180) of the Anglo-Saxon fyrd. By this Assize and its subsequent clarification and adaptation in later writs of Watch and Ward, culminating in the Statute of Winchester (1285), each man had to bear arms according to his rank and serve for wages when and where the king and council ordered him to go. These *jurati ad arma* were called out, though they never went into action, against Richard Marshal in 1233. A few hundred footmen were used in Henry III's campaigns in Brittany (1230) and Poitou (1242–3) and on the Welsh border about 1256, but these were all probably professionals, i.e. mercenaries. Simon de Montfort used a large force of Londoners at the battle of Lewes in 1264, and these sufficiently distracted the Lord Edward's attention to allow Simon to win the battle.

It is hard to say what part the enormous numbers of infantry summoned by Edward I played in the Scottish wars. For 1298 details are available. Three thousand men marched up from Snowdonia to Newcastle in thirteen days from Chester, and in another week's marching of 110 miles to Falkirk.[1] There were also another four thousand from Cheshire. These contingents averaged 15 to 20 miles a day—a remarkable feat for untrained soldiers.

---

[1] Details of the stages are given in H. Gough, *Scotland in 1298*. The relative importance of the knights may be instanced by the siege of Lochmaben Castle in September 1301 by 4 knights banneret, 240 men-at-arms, and 7,000 foot (Stevenson, *Docs.* ii. 421–5).

From the first the footmen were, like the fyrd, embodied by counties, by supervisors and later commissioners of array. A total of 25,000 men were called up from fifteen southern and eastern counties in 1295.[1] The *conductores* or colonels were mounted knights who led their chosen men of the shire to the mustering-point. In 1311 Sir Thomas Bardolf of Mapledurham Gurney, supervisor of array and conductor of the levies in Oxfordshire and Buckinghamshire, led his infantry to Roxburgh.[2] The infantry *Constable* was a heavy-armed cavalryman, a centurion who led a hundred footmen.[3] The Vintner was an N.C.O., the twentieth man leading nineteen others. The thirty constables who led the 3,000 foot from Snowdonia to Chester were under the care of three esquires or valets of the king's household (paid 1s. a day). The total wages bill of the infantry brigade from Chester to Newcastle in 1298 amounted to £342. 5s. 0d.

A glimpse behind the scenes is given in a letter dated at Glamorgan in 1316 to the king from his bachelor Sir William de Montague. 'I have found your bailiff of Gloucester has served you falsely, for where he should have brought 100 footmen he only brought 48, and these were of no value, and said before him that he had taken scot to leave the good ones at home.'

They then chose good constables in the presence of the sheriff, but when they came to Monmouth they brought 'worthless rascals, and took money to leave the good ones at home'.[4] This has been chosen as an illustration because the Parliament of Lincoln in January 1316 had granted the king one armed footman from every vill (though not on cities or boroughs on the royal demesne, which granted a fifteenth instead). These footmen had defensive armour

[1] *Parl. Writs*, i. 270.
[2] Ibid. ii. 479.
[3] Gough calls him a Captain, but in the thirteenth century a Captain was usually a much more important person, perhaps equivalent to a modern Major-General.
[4] *Cal. Chancery Warrants*, p. 437.

and were paid 4*d*. a day by the vill.[1] At an earlier date 'the court rolls seem to show that a village was ordered to produce a certain number of men, and these men were elected by their fellow villagers.[2] In one court, at Wakefield in 1295, it was found that Thomas Hull had gone round to each in turn of the men elected and persuaded each of them to pay him to do their military service for them in Wales. He then disappeared with the money.[3]

[1] 'Unum hominem peditem fortem et defensabilem', *Parl. Writs*, II. ii. 464, from Pat. Roll. The record known as the *Nomina Villarum* was compiled on this occasion, the vill being not necessarily a village, but the *villa integra* of royal records—an Exchequer administrative unit. See the note by B. Lees, '*Villa integra*', in *EHR*, xli (1926), 98–103.

[2] Homans, *The English Villager*, p. 329.   [3] Ibid., p. 330.

VII

CLIFFORD AGAIN

(I) CLIFFORD FROM 1298 TO 1308

IT is not always remembered that the numbers of troops engaged at Falkirk and at Caerlaverock were roughly the same. The Rolls of Arms give only the names of the bannerets—101 at Falkirk and 96 (+5 bachelors?) at Caerlaverock. But it must be obvious that bannerets are not found in isolation in any battle, and the *Song of Caerlaverock* states that Fitz-Marmaduke arrived with a great and full troop of good and choice bachelors.[1] A banneret may be expected, at this date, to lead a troop of thirty to fifty men-at-arms, and *Trois mil homes de arme gent*, that is, mounted troopers, are explicitly mentioned.[2] This is more than the 2,400 estimated to have fought at Falkirk.[3] The herald at Caerlaverock does in fact allude to 'countless bachelors'. The Earl of Hereford who led the second of the four brigades had 100 bachelors,[4] and the writer excuses himself for not being able to recall how many other bannerets there were. So, by implication, we may safely assume that the four brigades included 300 or 400 bachelors. The same is true of the four brigades at Falkirk, where in many cases we know the number of bachelors and esquires as well. The number of infantry ('pietaile') at Caerlaverock is quite unknown.[5]

[1] *Song*, ed. T. Wright, p. 28. Ralph de Gorges (no. 97) is described among the bannerets as a knight newly dubbed, i.e. he was knighted as a banneret, not as a bachelor. This can be paralleled from 1306.

[2] *Song*, pp. 26–27. *Gens d'armes* is a usual term at this period for cavalry.

[3] Sir Maurice Powicke, *The Thirteenth Century*, p. 693 n. 2, says that the Song about 'the brief siege of Caerlaverock has given the campaign an undeserved prominence in history'.

[4] *Song*, p. 5. The Galloway Roll of A.D. 1300 (Coll. of Arms MS. 14) lists 259 knights, banneret and bachelor.

[5] In the Stirling campaign of 1304 there were present and paid, at various

The strength of the garrison at Caerlaverock is un-known, but sixty men were left to surrender when the siege came to an end as their food ran out. From this point of view the situation of the Castle, protected by the con-fluence of the rivers Nith and Locker, about nine miles south of Dumfries, favoured the besiegers rather than the besieged, because before the siege was over the navy had arrived, as celebrated in the *Song*, to revictual them.

Clifford reappears on 4 June 1297 when he was em-powered with Percy to put down rebels within liberties and without and to do justice on them. The sheriffs of Lancashire, Westmorland, Cumberland, and Dumfries were to be intendent to them. They had received *viva voce* an overriding commission, superseding in practice the authority of Warenne and Cressingham.[1] On 12 July more detailed arrangements were made by which Clifford was appointed Captain of Cumberland, with Ralph Fitz-William and Brian Fitz-Alan for Northumberland.[2] On 24 September Clifford and Fitz-Alan were ordered to go to the help of Warenne, on 18 October they were again commissioned to defend the March, and on 14 November Clifford was empowered with the Bishop of Carlisle to receive Robert de Brus, Earl of Carrick, and his house-hold, into the king's peace, at discretion.[3]

At Falkirk, Sir Robert de Clifford, or Lord Robert Clifford, was a young banneret—he was 24 or 25—in the king's brigade (no. 56 on the roll), with a troop of eight knights, headed by Simon de Clifford, and twenty-six esquires, as his personal following. After the battle he made another contract with the king (25 November 1298) which put him in charge of Cumberland, Westmorland, Lancashire, and the valley of Annandale, and all the

dates, 5,000–7,000 footmen (Bain, *Cal. Docs. Scot.*). The foot at Falkirk were at least as numerous.

[1] Stevenson, ii. 170–3.
[2] Op. cit., p. 194 = *CPR*, p. 315.
[3] *Foed.* I. ii. 881. Percy and Warenne had gone south and were present at the Confirmation of the Charters in London (Morris, *Welsh Wars*, p. 284).

marches of those parts as far as the bounds of the county of Roxburgh.[1] Only a narrow strip of the lowlands approached by the Great North Road lay outside his jurisdiction. By this commission, all men-at-arms were to come to him at eight days' notice to Carlisle, and he would tell them what to do. This commission was more like that of Simon de Montfort's *custodes pacis*, or the Major-Generals with whom Sir Maurice Powicke has compared them, than the later commissions of Keepers or Justices of the Peace. Thus by the time of Caerlaverock Clifford and Percy were the two most powerful men on the Border.[2] Hence if Percy appears at Falkirk with a King of Arms in his train, it is likely that Clifford, too, had one, if not at Falkirk, certainly at Caerlaverock. The *Song*, with its eulogy of Clifford, who was given charge of the Castle when it surrendered, may have been composed by a herald brought back from Flanders in 1297. The language of the *Song* is northern French.

The passage runs:

> Robert le seignour de Cliffort[3]
> A ki raisons donne confort
> De ses enemis encombrer
> Toutes le foiz ki remembrer
> Ki puet de son noble lignage.
> Escoce pregn à tesmoignage,

[1] *Foed.* I. ii. 901. Clifford's commission gave him power 'sur totes les gentz darmes, e de chose qe touche fet de armes, de gent a chival e a pee', with power to distrain and punish. It is a purely military commission, but it will be remembered that he was already hereditary sheriff of Westmorland.

[2] The *Liber Quotidianus* of the Wardrobe (p. 189) records Clifford's payment at Kirkcudbright as a king's banneret for June–August 1300, i.e. during the siege of Caerlaverock.

[3] *Song*, pp. 11–12. Clifford is no. 40 in the *Song*. The arms are also in Collins' Roll no. 23, Falkirk no. 55, PRA 38, and Dunstable (Warwick retinue) no. 47. Four of his knights were Dumfriesshire men. One of them, Tateshal, also had a chequey coat, as also had the Earl of Warwick, who on Clifford's death had (August 1315) the custody of his lands. Both Clifford and Warwick were hereditary sheriffs, accounting at the Exchequer, and there is possibly an allusion to this in the arms. Warwick's arms were chequey *Or* and *Az.* a chevron *Erm.* (e.g. Collins' no. 7).

Ki ben e noblement commence,
Cum cil ki est de la semence
Le Conte Mareschal le noble,
Ki par dela Constantinoble
A l'unicorn se combati
E desouz di mort le abati.
De li de par mere est venus
A ki fu ben pareil tenus,
Li bons Rogers, pere son pere;

.   .   .   .

Sa baniere mout honourée,
De or e de asur eschequeré,
O une fesse vermellette.
Si je estoie une pucellette,
Je li donroie quer e cors.
Tant est de li bons li recors.

As the hero of one Roll of Arms and possibly the instigator of another, Clifford is worth all our attention.
At the time of Falkirk he had been a Warden of the
March of Scotland.[1] On 17 August 1299 his contract was
running out, but in January 1300 he agreed to stay on till
Michaelmas under John de St. John *le père*,[2] hence his
presence at Caerlaverock, but he did not long remain
governor of that Castle, being appointed Constable of
Nottingham in September of the same year.[3] In this
appointment he was confirmed on 20 August 1307.[4] He
had presumably been at the Feast on 22 May 1306, for
he is reported to have gone north with Henry Percy and
the Prince thereafter.[5] He served at this time in his own
March under Percy, who was made Lieutenant for the
whole of Lancashire, Westmorland, Cumberland, and
Galloway, with Carlisle as his headquarters. This is very
odd, for at Berwick, where we might rather have expected

---

[1] For his position 1298–9 as Captain of the defence in the parts of Carlisle and
King's Lieutenant there, see *CPR*, pp. 392, 409.

[2] Bain, ii. 276, 287. He had employed an Irish Hobelar as a spy (ibid., p. 275).

[3] Ibid., p. 294.   [4] *CFR*, ii. 2.

[5] Hem., p. 248; Trivet, p. 409; *Flores*, p. 131.

Percy, Valence was made Lieutenant for Yorkshire, North-umberland, and Lothian as far as Dumfries.[1] Clifford was at Carlisle on 28 January 1307,[2] and was too much oc-cupied to be at the Parliament of Carlisle at that time.[3] He was on the Border, at or near Ayr, some time between July and August 1307,[4] but we do not know the terms of his service. It is therefore not impossible that he attended the death-bed of Edward I, there to receive, so the story runs, an injunction to prevent the return to England, which he failed to do, of the recently exiled Piers Gaveston.[5]

Clifford came south to become acting Marshal of Eng-land at the beginning of Edward II's reign.[6] This office he held from about 3 September 1307 until March 1308, when he surrendered this office together with that of Justice of the Forest, North of Trent.[7]

The actual day of Clifford's appointment as acting Marshal is uncertain. He was certainly in office by the time of the fateful tournament at Wallingford in Decem-ber 1307, which the king had attended, and he cannot escape responsibility for the organization of the Corona-tion in February 1308. These two events alone would account for his retirement in March.

(ii) THE NATIVITY ROLL

On the dorse of the Falkirk Roll was written a list of seventy-nine knights headed by a statement that they were present on 'Monday before the Nativity of Our Lady' on some occasion thought worthy of record by a herald, for

---

[1] *Cal. Cl. R.*, pp. 432–3; *CPR*, p. 426.
[2] PRO E. 101/369/11, fol. 198ᵛ, includes a note of 50 marks paid to him.
[3] *Cal. Cl. R.*, p. 486.   [4] Bain, ii, no. 1961.
[5] See 'The Tournament in England', in *Essays Presented to Sir F. M. Powicke* (1948), p. 268, and *DNB*, s.v. Beauchamp, Guy de.
[6] Clifford was never (*pace* DNB) 'Earl Marshal'. The Marshalship in fee was vacant between the death of Roger Bigod in 1306 and the creation of Thomas de Brotherton as Earl of Norfolk in 1312.
[7] He had also been guardian of the liberty of the Bishopric of Durham while Bek was in exile (*CFR*, ii. 2).

the coats of arms are given.[1] What feat of arms is celebrated we are not told. It might have been merely a Round Table, perhaps to celebrate the settlement of Scotland in September 1305, but this date is impossible because at least seventeen of the persons named had been knighted at the Feast of the Swans at Westminster on 22 May 1306, so that the Feast of the Nativity mentioned in the roll must be not earlier than the first week in September 1306. Now Greenstreet had already shown that the limits of date, on genealogical grounds, were 1299–1309, and was himself inclined to give as the date a year or two earlier than the close of Edward's reign. He noted that John de Mowbray (no. 2) was only 19 in 1306. To this I may add that the use of labels necessitates a date before that of the First Dunstable Roll (1309), so that the Nativity Roll may now be dated in the first week of September 1306, 1307, or 1308.

The provenance of the roll suggests some north-country connexion, and it is found that many of the seventy-nine were northerners by birth. Presumably some of them went north with the king or the prince on that last journey to Scotland after the murder of Comyn in February 1306 and the consequent Feast of the Swans where Edward I swore to take his revenge upon the Scots, and some of the young men had been knighted at Westminster.

The Nativity Roll could thus be for a Round Table at or near Lanercost, where the king was staying in September 1306. There was at this time another offer for young men to be knighted by the king in person, and traces of this have survived in the additions at the end of the PRA of the investiture of new knights in October–November 1306. In a normal roll of this length we should expect to find at least ten bannerets, but I cannot here name more than two. Furthermore, this number of bachelors in a military action would imply a total cavalry force of some

[1] The Nativity Roll is well edited by James Greenstreet in *The Reliquary*, xv (1875), 27–32, 68–74, from Harl. MS. 6589, fol. 9–9ᵛ. See *CEMRA*, pp. 27, 35–36.

400 men, and of this there is no trace. For lack of evidence no more can be said than that this was probably a Round Table or jollification during a lull in the fighting in September 1306, 1307, or 1308.[1]

(III) LABELS

The use of labels as marks of cadency is well illustrated by a comparison of their occurrence in the arms of Latimer in the Nativity Roll, the Falkirk Roll, and the Dunstable Roll. The net result, historically speaking, is to show that the Nativity Roll is to be dated before the Dunstable Roll of July (?) 1309 and after 1305, because William le Latimer le filz changed his arms on the death of his father in that year. From this, and the inclusion of seventeen 'Swan Knights', we arrive at the conclusion that the feast of the Nativity of Our Lady, mentioned in the mutilated heading of the roll, was that celebrated on 9 September 1306, 1307, or 1308. Greenstreet, seeing the possibility of this argument, though he did not elaborate it, made a shrewd guess at the date.

The labels in question may be thus displayed:

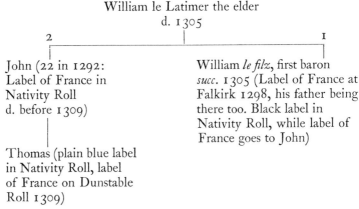

William le Latimer the elder
d. 1305

2   1

John (22 in 1292:   William *le filz*, first baron
Label of France in   *succ.* 1305 (Label of France at
Nativity Roll   Falkirk 1298, his father being
d. before 1309)   there too. Black label in
                                    Nativity Roll, while label of
                                    France goes to John)

Thomas (plain blue label
in Nativity Roll, label
of France on Dunstable
Roll 1309)

---

[1] There *was* a Round Table at Falkirk in the Octave of St. Hilary, 1302 (Chron. Ed. I and II (*Ann. Lond.*), i. 104).

This is the only descent of the period in which the use of labels is so clearly shown in a well developed and systematic fashion.

Labels are numerous on the Dunstable Roll, as might be expected on any tournament roll, where the combatants would tend to belong to the younger generation. This is also noticeable on the Nativity Roll, but there are very few on the PRA. At Dunstable 12 of the 70 comprising the *Commune* bore arms with labels; 9 in Lancaster's troop, 2 with Warenne, but none with Arundel or Hereford. Theobald of Verdun has a label at Falkirk (1298) but has dropped it in PRA. Bartholomew de Badlesmere has a blue label at Caerlaverock (1300) but not at Dunstable (1309).

On the other hand Henry Fitz Hugh bore a red label of three points on the Dunstable Roll (no. 38) but not on PRA 130, which, if taken as decisive, would place the PRA after July 1309, unless there were, as is possible, two Henrys in succession. And 'John de Hastings' has a label on PRA 978 (Staffs.) but not on Dunstable (no. 207). 'John' may well be two people. But though the PRA is clearly the greatest and most authoritative of these rolls, the unique contemporary manuscript has not the appearance of an 'original copy'.

Having established the use of labels at the end of the century, we revert to Glover's Roll and Matthew Paris[1] to show that this usage was already in being about 1252. The Matthew Paris shields[2] include labels (*lambelli*) for John de Berners, the Earl of Lincoln, Richard de Montfichet, and William de Valence, son of the Count de la Marche.[3]

[1] *Supra*, p. 42.

[2] The shields described and painted by Matthew Paris are conveniently brought together in vol. vi, app. i, pp. 469–77 of H. R. Luard's edition of the *Chronica Majora*. See further *CEMRA*, pp. 1–3 and plate I.

[3] *Not* William the bishop-elect of Valence.

VIII

THE CONSTABLE, THE MARSHAL, AND THE *CURIA MILITARIS*

ALL constables in thirteenth-century England had some disciplinary powers. Whether it is the Constable of England, or the local Constables of the Peace, the Constables who led the infantry in war or the Constables of Castles, they were all in some sense leaders of the flock, responsible (as Constable of England) for the payment of stipendiaries and for the discipline of the troops under his command, or (as local Constable of hundreds) for the pursuit and detention of criminals with the aid of the *posse comitatus* if necessary. The Constable of England, or the Lord High Constable of England, to give him his sixteenth-century title, is in the *Dialogus de Scaccario* of Henry II's reign the *miles gregarius*—the leader of the flock, possibly the 'Chief Buzo' like the *bucc' gregis* of *Fleta*, who is a local dignitary.

The position of the Constable in the latter part of the twelfth century is obscure,[1] though the right to the office was already in the Bohun family.[2] The office was in effect

[1] For the twelfth-century constables see J. H. Round, *The King's Serjeants*, pp. 63, 79–82, and *Addenda*; the same author's *Peerage and Pedigree*, i. 151–2. For the Norman period see G. H. White in G.E.C. *Complete Peerage*, vol. x, app. F, pp. 67–69 (cf. vol. vi, s.v. Hereford), and the same author on 'Coronation Claims' in *The Genealogical Magazine*, vii. 510 seq., and on 'Constables under the Norman Kings', op. cit., N.S., vol. 38 (1922), pp. 113–27. Mr. Charles Johnson's luciferous account of the early descent of the office is in his edition of the *Dialogus de Scaccario* (Nelson, 1950), pp. xxxii–xxxiii, which supersedes the Oxford edition of 1902. The history of the Bohun family in the *fundatorum progenies* printed by Dugdale in his *Mon. Ang.* (old ed.), ii. 66–68, and relied upon in his *Baronage*, i. 179, has been responsible for much error.

[2] In 1229 Earl Humphrey was granted the arrears of his accustomed fees from the time of Henry II (*Cl. R.*, p. 223). His father Henry also had £20 p.a. in 1205 *nomine Comitis*, i.e. the third penny of the pleas of the county (*R. lit. cl.*, 22 March 1205, p. 23).

suppressed by John, but comes fully into view with Humphrey (V) de Bohun (1220–75), who exercised his right of
presenting a deputy at the Exchequer in 1228. His
father Henry had put the family in the front rank of the
baronage by his marriage with Geoffrey de Mandeville's
daughter, so that Humphrey, Earl of Hereford, was also
after 1236 Earl of Essex. From this time the Constable's
deputies in the Exchequer can easily be traced,[1] and from
this time the office is clearly hereditary in the Bohun
family.

The Constable and the Marshal each had deputies at
the Exchequer and the army in the field, but unlike the
Marshal the Constable had no deputies in the royal
household. With the creation of the Exchequer the Constable 'went out of Court', though still entitled to *bouche
à court* when he attended.[2] He therefore lost the day-to-day
opportunity, retained by the Marshal, of initiating in-
trigues within the household, as in 1234.[3] As paymaster-
general the Constable took 2*d.* in the pound on those
wages for which he was responsible.[4] But as he was no
longer intimately associated with the daily business of
the king—though he is in the *Constitutio Domus Regis* of
Henry I's reign and there is much about him in the *Dialogus de Scaccario* (where he is the *miles gregarius*)[5]—he is not

---

[1] T. Madox, *History of the Exchequer* (ed. 1711), pp. 556, 564, 724–5; Conway
Davies, *Baronial Opposition to Edward II*, pp. 312–13.

[2] Humphrey de Bohun took 5*s.* a day when he did not eat in Court, and 3*s.* 6*d.*
only when he did, *pro feudo suo*, from 23 July *anno presenti* (? 1306), on which
day the Constable and Marshal first took their fee by ordinance of King and
Council, down to 1 September, *quo die dominus rex rediit de guerra sua* (Droxford's
account book, PRO E. 101/373/15, p. 10).

[3] The dismissal of Sir William de Rodune, Kt., the Marshal's deputy at court
in 1234, who was unacceptable to Henry III, is said by Roger Wendover to have
occasioned the rebellion of the Young Marshal.

[4] This appears from an inquiry made in 1282 (*Foed.*, p. 615, cf. Morris,
Welsh Wars, pp. 155–6, 196). But there is a bond to Roger le Bigot [etc.] in
£38. 12*s.* 8*d.* of the monies of the marshalcy of the said earl which were with-
drawn from the wages of knights and sergeants for the time they were on the
king's service in Gascony (*CPR*, 1247–58, p. 394 (18 January 1255)).

[5] The Constable's deputies in the field were called *Duces militum* in the Poitou
campaign of 1242. Paulinus Piper (q.v.) was one of four (*Foed.*, p. 248 = *CPR*,

mentioned in the Household Ordinances of 1318 and 1323. These abound with information about knight marshals and sergeant marshals and the Marshalsea Court for debtors.[1]

For the Constable, the break with the court is clear by 1228, when Earl Humphrey de Bohun is described as *Constabularius Regis de scaccario*, on presenting a deputy.[2]

As *miles gregarius* it may be thought that he is better described as 'leader of the flock' than by the classical translation 'common soldier'. As such he was responsible for the discipline of the army, working with the Marshal. The Welsh in the army in Gascony in 1254 were severely punished by the king's brothers for making a raid without first consulting the Constable. Hereford complained to the king, who merely laughed at him.[3]

The style Constable of England is rarely found in the thirteenth century. It has been noticed in 1275 and 1301.[4]

Unlike the Constable, the Marshal never deserted the Court for the Exchequer: though he had his deputies everywhere—in the household, the Exchequer, the central courts of law, and in his own prison, the Fleet. He was responsible jointly with the Steward for the Court of the Verge (the Palace court).[5]

p. 302). They too, therefore, might be called leaders of the flock, like the local constables in England who led the hue and cry. It may be that these latter are the *bucc' gregis* of *Fleta* (c. 1290). The local constables, that is the hundred (or chief) constables of 1242, a development from the *milites assignati* of 1195, pursued, caught, and handed over for trial such criminals as came their way, and also mustered the *jurati ad arma*. They are the predecessors of the Keepers of the Peace (see the paper by Alan Harding in *T. R. Hist. Soc.* (1960), 'The Origins and Early History of the Keepers of the Peace', pp. 85–109). This view of Constables suggests a new line of inquiry into the still vexed *Buzones* (see G. Lapsley in *EHR* (1947), pp. 177–93, 545–67), in which connexion a passage in *PQW*, p. 407b, about persons who ought not to be amerced with the shire because they were not accustomed to be present at false judgements, may turn out to be of particular relevance.

[1] The Constable is not mentioned in the chapter on the Wardrobe and Household in *The King's Government at Work, 1327–1337*, ed. Willard and Morris.
[2] Madox, *Hist. of the Exchequer*, p. 724 (from the Close Roll), which see for some thirteenth-century deputies.   [3] Matt. Par., *Chron. Maj.* v, pp. 442–3.
[4] *CFR* (1275), p. 52, and the letter to the Pope of 1301 (*Foed.*, p. 936).
[5] The author of *Fleta* had access to these rolls for 19 Ed. I, which he cites.

The connexion between the Constable and the Marshal was very close in time of war. They acted jointly and by deputy in guarding prisoners and surrendered castles. The garrison of Stirling Castle, after the siege in 1304, was handed over to Sir John Lovel, the deputy Constable, and the Marshal's deputy was to guard the prisoners.[1] The Marshal's harbingers arranged lodgings for the court on all its travels, and for the cavalry (at least) at Caerlaverock. The Marshal received the custody of the Castle at the end of the siege. The Constable's deputies gave certificates of military service performed. Nicholas Segrave, who became deputy marshal at court in 1308 (after Clifford), was Bohun's lieutenant as Constable at Caerlaverock, and as deputy constable certified that Henry de Middelton had personally his banner there on 14 July 1300 by witness of Sir William de Felton.[2] As Middelton is not in the *Song* this seems to mean that he was a standard-bearer, not that he was himself a banneret.

In the first extant roll of 'Pleas of the Army' in Edward I's reign,[3] the Marshal (Sir John Lovel) appears as an active disciplinary official. He and his bailiff were active in dealing with theft and pillaging by the troops, and in pacifying the Welsh. Similar Pleas of the Army before the Constable and the Marshal were heard at Tutbury in 1322.[4] The concurrent jurisdiction of the Constable and the Marshal was similarly exercised in this year in Roger Damory's trial for treason, held before the deputy Constable, Fulk FitzWarin, and the deputy Marshal, John de Weston.[5] From the time of Edward I the Civil Law was applied in treason cases.[6]

In Edward I's time the business of the heralds at tournaments, and the whole conduct of these affairs, was supervised by commissions set up in 1265 and 1293 under

---

[1] *Foed.* I. ii. 965.
[2] Stevenson, *Docs.* (1870), pp. 415–16.
[3] Bain, *CDS*, ii. 189–91.
[4] *Parl. Writs*, II. ii, App. 260.
[5] *Chron. Ed. I & II* (RS), i. 139.
[6] See Kean, op. cit., in *T. R. Hist. Soc.* (1962).

the *Statutum Armorum*,[1] but in these the Constable does not appear—his ancestors had gone 'out of court', though he could still appear and eat there. In the period covered by the Rolls of Arms down to 1322 the Constable had nothing whatever to do with Heralds in the history or literature of England.[2]

The lack of any evidence for the existence of a court dealing with heraldry as well as tournaments in the thirteenth century is a matter for surprise, because even at that date coats of arms were disputed,[3] and all great tenants-in-chief had their own 'knighten courts' or *Curie militum* (i.e. honour courts, often so styled)—as at Skipton Castle and Carisbroke Castle. These fall naturally under the presidency of the local Constable or Steward, but in none of them is there any trace of heraldic activity.

We leave the heralds in 1318, still in the Marshal's department, and therefore subject to the old Lancastrian claims as Steward of the Household, which may explain what happened in 1347. But the position of the heralds in the later middle ages is bedevilled by Lancastrian intrigue, and in the fifteenth century by a temporary arrogation of the Marshal's function by the Constable. With the Tudors and the first heraldic visitations matters reverted to normal.[4]

---

[1] See 'The Tournament in the Thirteenth Century' cited above.

[2] When a heraldic dispute did occur in 1347 before Calais, it was heard by the Earl of Lancaster, as Steward of England, under a Commission to hear all disputes touching Arms.

[3] Wagner, *Heralds and Heraldry*, pp. 19, 21, 122.

[4] See for the later Court of Chivalry Mr. G. D. Squibb's work under that title (1959), but this entertaining and valuable work throws no light on the history of heralds or heraldry in our period.

IX

THE DUNSTABLE TOURNAMENT ROLL

THE Dunstable tournament of 1309 is a most striking manifestation of the increasing lawlessness of the decade that culminated in the Ordinances of 1310. The mounting tide of local disorder, traceable in the chancery records, pointed to social evils more usually associated with the period of Lancastrian decline. The root of the evil was the breakdown of old methods of enforcing the peace—the frankpledge system and Watch and Ward and local constables backed up by periodical judicial eyres. This led to 'maintenance' and the prevalence of 'vagabonds and *those who hire them to maltreat and kill others*' in fairs, markets, and other places out of hatred, envy, or malice, or because of being put on assizes, juries, and inquisitions, whereby the latter dare not tell the truth; touching those who give gifts to and maintain[1] malefactors; those who by reason of their power and lordship, take any persons into their protection and advowson, and who extort money by threats'. This is the picture given in the writs that provided the remedy, according to an Ordinance made by the King and Council in Parliament[2] or (14 Oct. 1305) 'made by King and Council delivered to the judges in parliament'.[3]

The Ordinances referred to were intended, as it were, to bring the King's Court into the shires, by enlarging the powers of the justices of *Oyer et Terminer*.[4] The new justices, called by the chroniclers judges of Trailbaston,

---

[1] For six London citizens accused of maintenance in 1305 see *CPR*, p. 372.
[2] *CPR* (1305), p. 352.
[3] Ibid., p. 404.
[4] *Cal. Chancery Warrants*, p. 250.

were to present a long series of articles to a jury of 12 in each vill, and to imprison the offenders.[1]

In the last years of the reign there were a vast number of such commissions and the outlawry procedure was used on a large scale.[2]

It was partly the king's own fault that matters had reached such a pitch, as the old procedure for outlawry of criminals had quite broken down, and large numbers had been pardoned and released for military service in and after 1297. In 1306 sixty persons were pardoned for outlawry on non-appearance before the justices, and there were at least as many more such pardons that do not specify military service.[3] The Scottish wars were largely to blame: the barons deserted to tourney while lesser folk took to crime. Thomas of Lancaster himself, who had livery of his estates in 1298, though he was probably only twenty, two years after his father's death in Gascony, had already by 1305 indulged in a whole series of outrages in the course of a private war with the Prior of Tutbury.[4] Yet on 4 November 1306 he was pardoned all his debts to the Exchequer for his services in Scotland—a polite way, perhaps, of expressing the king's gratitude to Edmund his father.[5]

There was, too, much local rioting and destruction of property while the owners were away on service, a feature that could be fully illustrated in the last years of Edward I's reign and throughout the reign of Edward II. The long lists of accused in each single action show plainly that rioting on a considerable scale is frequently the issue,

---

[1] Hem., pp. 235–41; *Rot. Parl.* i. 18; *Parl. Writs*, i. 408; *Flores*, iii. 122–3; *Ann. Wigorn.*, p. 557; Rishanger, p. 224; *Ann. Lond.*, p. 134; Trevet, p. 404.

[2] The earliest Trailbaston commission, i.e. *Oyer et Terminer*, with the addition of a 'hiring and beating' clause seems to be in *CPR* (1301–7), pp. 354 (6 April 1305), 547. In that volume some commissions are styled *Oyer et Terminer* in the text of the calendar, but indexed under *Trailbaston*.

[3] Between November 1306 and July 1307 there were approximately 100 pardons for outlawry before the justices of *Oyer et Terminer*, apart from the sixty mentioned above.

[4] *CPR*, pp. 353, 405–6.   [5] Ibid., p. 468.

not individual crime, e.g. breaking into parks, destroying a record office, assaulting an unpopular Dean, or breaking into the Archbishop's palace at Canterbury, or 'cutting into small pieces and sinking the Earl of Gloucester's ships while he was in Scotland in 1301'.[1] This general spirit of lawlessness was soon to find a focus in the baronial hostility to the young king's favourite, Piers Gaveston.

The opening years of the reign of Edward II are of great importance in the history of heraldry. The heralds themselves cannot be traced in the records, but some of the results of their activities may still be read in the two contemporary and authoritative blazoned rolls, one probably from the court (the Parliamentary Roll of Arms) and one (the First Dunstable Roll) which is more or less a list of the incipient Lancastrian faction on a war footing. Political events illuminate these rolls and in return receive some light from them. On the one hand the hostility of the earls to the young king and his favourites found a natural focus in the tournament at Dunstable in 1309. On the other, the hostility of the régime to Droxford and Benstede, both gentlemen of coat-armour who ranked as bannerets in the royal household and had fought with their retinues in Flanders in 1297 and at Falkirk in 1298, is indicated by their absence from the PRA, in which Gaveston and Cornwall are to the fore, while Lancaster is relegated to the end.[2]

Gaveston is thought to have come to England with his father Arnald de Gaveston in 1299 and had been Edward's

___

[1] *CPR* (1301–7), pp. 78 (Earl of Gloucester), 198 (the Dean of Selling), 278 (Archbishop of Canterbury), 275 (the sub-escheator's record office in Berkshire).

[2] The opposition to Droxford and Benstede perhaps crystallized in 1306, when they had been responsible for the imprisonment of deserters from the army, who indulged in tournaments when they should have been in Scotland. The list of names reveals in a small way the degree of opposition that existed to the Scottish war. The twenty-two baronial deserters included Gaveston, Gilbert de Clare, Roger Mortimer, and Tony, all members of the prince's household. All their lands were to be seized, and Droxford was ordered to lock them up, but three months later (23 January 1307) most of them were pardoned at the instance of the queen (*CFR*, i. 543–4; *Cal. Cl. R.*, pp. 481–2).

boyhood companion, but was banished from the court in 1305, though the prince implored his sister, the Lady Elizabeth, to persuade the king to let him have 'Perot' with him. The prince too was banished from the court for four months in the Parliament of 1305, because of his violent language to the Treasurer, Walter Langton, who would not condone his extravagance. Matters came to a head with Gaveston's desertion from the army in 1306 and his banishment from the country (18 October 1306) with a pension of 100 marks a year from Gascon revenues, for as long as he remained abroad.[1] But on the old king's death he immediately returned and was at once made Earl of Cornwall on the accession of Edward II. He received not only the vast estates which had been accumulated by Richard, King of the Romans,[2] but much of the Fortibus-Redvers inheritance as well. He held, in a word, the whole body of estates that a few years later became the endowment of the King's Chamber, including Holderness, Skipton, the Peak (a Ferrers, Earl of Derby, forfeiture), Cockermouth, the Isle of Wight,[3] as well as Cornwall, Wallingford, Berkhamsted, and the Isle of Man,[4] though not Devon.[5]

The political hostility to Gaveston lay partly in antagonisms that had been carried over from the reign of Edward I. His chief opponents were, however, to be not in the civil servants but in the baronage. Their hostility to his creation as Earl of Cornwall on 7 August 1307 was intensified by his marriage on 3 November 1307 at Berkhamsted to Margaret de Clare.[6] This seemed likely to perpetuate his

---

[1] See the letters in W. H. Blaauw, *Sussex Arch. Soc.* ii. 82–97; *Parl. Writs*, i. 378–80; *Foed.* i. 1010.

[2] See my *Richard of Cornwall*, pp. 162–70.

[3] See my *Seignorial Administration in England*, chap. i.

[4] See Dugdale, *Baronage*, ii. 41.

[5] The earldom of Devon was vacant from 1293 till 1336.

[6] The place of Gaveston's marriage is known from a version of Higden's 'Polychronicon' in Bod. Lib. MS. Laud Misc. 529, cited by Dugdale in his *Baronage*, ii (1676), p. 42, col. 1, as Bod. Lib. K. 84, fol. 93a. (This is not in the printed Higden (RS 41, vol. viii) and has eluded *DNB* and G.E.C.) The date is

intrusion into the charmed circle of the aristocracy—
for the earls, few as they were, could still be regarded as
almost a separate estate of the realm, superior in kind
as well as degree to the rest of the baronage.

The acquisition of the earldom of Cornwall involved
large territorial agglomerations, including the honours
of Wallingford and St. Valery, the two great castles of
Wallingford and Berkhamsted, and, in effect, the control
of the Thames valley in partnership with Windsor. The
political repercussions of this marriage were great. But
Gaveston's elevation might have been forgiven if not forgotten, had he not had the luck or folly to defeat the
barons at their own game—at his tournament at Wallingford on 2 December 1307. This earned him the undying
enmity of the magnates.[1] It was, indeed the *fons et origo* of
baronial hatred of Gaveston because he had there routed
the earls with his troop of young foreign upstarts. To
make matters worse Gaveston had been left in England as
Regent (18 January 1308) with 'unusually wide powers',
and thus given an opportunity of consolidating the position that he had so suddenly acquired. It must be urged
in his favour that he did not abuse his authority: he was
never an unconstitutional favourite; merely a vain and at
times frivolous one with a waspish tongue, but a good
jouster and, in Ireland at least, a competent administrator.

fixed thus: Piers Gaveston *and Margaret his wife* are mentioned in a writ of
26 June 1308 (*Cal. IPM*, vol. v, no. 73) referring to the grant to Piers and
Margaret his wife of the Honour of Skipton, before the death of Everard de
Fauvel (whose *IPM* this is). Now the marriage took place in the presence of the
king, according to the chronicle, and between his accession and 26 June 1308
Edward is known to have been there only once, i.e. 2–3 November 1307 (*CPR*,
pp. 10, 11, 37). His next visit, on 4–9 August 1308, was perhaps to see to the
safe custody of the place during Gaveston's exile in Ireland (*CPR*, 136; *C. Ch. R.*,
p. 121). On the first occasion Henry de Lacy obtained a mortmain licence for
his new foundation, Lincoln College, at Oxford, and at the same time the
attack on Edward I's fallen minister, Walter Langton, was initiated by a
commission to inquire into his encroachments as Master of the Hospital of
St. Leonard's, York.

[1] The Wallingford tournament is sometimes misdated by modern writers.
That it took place on 2 December is stated in *Vita Edwardi*, p. 2.

Clifford did nothing to remedy a situation for which he must bear some responsibility, by reason of his position as Marshal, if not for the sake of any promise made to the dead king. He resigned at the insistence of the magnates in March 1308 at the Council of Northampton and joined, if he had not already done so, the Earl of Warwick's retinue. Clifford is spoken of as a moderate man, and his private life attracted no unfavourable comment. His choice of a patron might seem an odd one, but there seems to be no solid ground on which to base an attack on Warwick at this time. The murder of Gaveston was still in the future, and a contemporary defence of Earl Guy has been neglected.[1]

Clifford, as Marshal, permitted the vulgar ostentation of Piers Gaveston at the Coronation on 25 February 1308. He had been a party to the obscure letters patent issued in French and sealed at Boulogne on 31 January[2] by Lincoln, Warenne, Hereford, Robert Clifford, Payn Tibetot, Henry de Gray, John Botetourt, and John of Berwick. Their declared object was 'to preserve his [the King's] honour and the rights of his Crown', in order to do which they also agreed *'les choses que sount feites avant ces houres countre soen honeur, et le droit de sa coroune, et les oppressiouns que ount esté feit et uncore se fount de jour en jour a soen people de redresser et mettre pour amendement'* &c. Each and all swore to this, and Bek was to have power of excommunication if any one of them broke his oath.

The awkwardness of the phrasing shows the difficulty they found in feeling their way to that famous fourth clause added a few weeks later to the Coronation Oath. For there is nothing about *obeying the* LAWS *chosen by the Community*, with its parallel ambiguity in *chosen*, which might mean existing or future legislation. But they make

---

[1] *Vita Edwardi*, p. 28.

[2] Dr. R. W. Hunt, the Keeper of Western MSS., very kindly supplied me with a transcript of this document which was copied by Dugdale into his MS. 18, fol. 80, in the Bodleian Library, from a manuscript of Robert Glover.

it clear that if given the chance their action will be retro-spective, and so we may if we wish interpret the Corona-tion Oath of 1308 in the light of this document, but with the unhappy result of emphasizing the ambiguity as to the extent to which they are determined to bridle the king.

The Coronation Oath was much in the air at this time, and the idea was current that the *tria precepta* of the oath—to keep peace with the Church and all Christian peoples, to repress crime, and to do justice—were insufficient. Under canonical influence[1] the idea had grown up that 'the king was not only bound to maintain the rights of the Crown, but should swear to do so at the coronation'.[2] Mr. Richardson has shown that Henry III and Edward I did so swear and that on nine formal occasions Edward I put it in writing that he had so sworn, and on the first of these occasions, in 1275, he added that he could do nothing touching the Crown without the consent of his barons.

It was a determination to have this point made clear that induced Anthony Bek's party to issue their manifesto; and it was in fact incorporated as a fourth clause in the oath sworn by Edward II, in a strongly baronial form. The fourth clause was inserted, we are told, not as an attack upon Gaveston, but as a bridle upon the king.

It is probable that the guarded wording of the Oath is meant to include the possibility that if Edward II turned out to be as foolish a king as everyone had a right to fear from his behaviour as prince, each would know upon whom he could rely. But we cannot exclude the possibility that it is merely the immediate baronial reaction to the unusual position accorded to a foreign upstart, for Gaves-ton had been appointed Regent on 18 January, and these men had gone with Edward to Boulogne to assist at his marriage and bring home his young French wife Isabella, the French king's daughter.

---

[1] E. Kantorowicz on 'Inalienability', in *Speculum* (1954), vol. xxix.

[2] H. G. Richardson, 'The English Coronation Oath', in *Speculum* (1949), vol. xxix.

It may be significant that less than half the baronage (seventy-two of them) were summoned individually to the Coronation, which was set back a week from the day originally intended.[1] The invitations were sent out on 8 February 1308, and on the 9th a tournament was prohibited at Croydon or elsewhere before the Coronation.[2] On the 25th, the very day of the ceremony, a writ was issued prohibiting a tournament on an unspecified date. This has been taken to mean that a tournament had been arranged in advance to be held on the day of the Coronation,[3] but such an unprecedented event would certainly have incurred far harsher treatment, and the futility of issuing a writ of such immediacy would have been apparent. It may be doubted whether political feeling had yet reached such a pitch of fever that the opposition would propose a demonstration in force, before the new king had had a chance to show whether he could rule as well as reign. That the barons who were not summoned to the Coronation held meetings of their own may well be, but there is no record that they did so or even that they proposed to do so.

An attempt to win a wider basis of support for the king may be seen in the permissive writs to the sheriffs for local knights to be invited to the Coronation accompanied by their wives. This may have been usual, though I do not know of any earlier invitations to ladies on such occasions: but it was done while Gaveston was regent, and for the writs of 8 February he was responsible, i.e. the series beginning 'William de Leybourne and his wife'.[4] Was it perhaps Gaveston's own idea? At the ceremony itself his presumption in taking precedence immediately after the

[1] The invitations are in *Foed.* and *Parl. Writs*, but I cannot find any second series of writs postponing the ceremony from 18 to 25 February. The existing writs are dated 18 January and 8 February at Dover (*Cal. Cl. R.*, p. 51; *Foed.* ii. i. 27), and the postponement is known only from the Annals of London.

[2] *Cal. Cl. R.*, p. 52.

[3] T. F. Tout, *Political History of England (1216–1377)*, p. 239.

[4] Efforts were made to bring Archbishop Winchelsey back from exile for the Coronation (*Foed.* ii. 92) but they were too late to be effective.

king caused great baronial indignation.[1] Whether by acci-
dent or design he fared almost as well in the PRA.

A much noticed passage in the *Vita Edwardi* styles
Gaveston *camerarius*, an office—if office is meant—to which
he had no right and laid no claim. The implications of the
phrase are obvious. The Marshalship in fee was vacant
after December 1306. Clifford, the acting Marshal, was
dismissed in March 1308 and his successor Nicholas Segrave suffered a similar fate in August, by temporary ex-
pulsion from the court, though he did not, we are told, lose
the office (cf. William de Rodune in 1233). Edward II was
now to all intents and purposes his own Marshal. It is
precisely at this point that Gaveston occurs as *camerarius*.
It may be suggested that he was usurping the Marshal's
position at coronations and tournaments and over the
heralds by attracting the Marshal's authority out of the
Hall into the Chamber, though he had no official position
there. This might be one of the seeds that burgeoned in
the Chamber a few years later, when the Privy Seal in
1312 was made a public department and the king maintained the sanctity of his household and the efficacy of his
power by extending the authority and resources of his
Chamber. It was in the king's chamber, at any rate, that
Gaveston lived and had his influence,[2] and from this
vantage-point he could have arranged the Wallingford
tournament or set on foot the compilation of a Roll of
Arms with his own name second only to Gloucester after
the king. This would explain, then, some curious features
of the PRA, the use of the word *camerarius* in the *Vita
Edwardi*, and the failure to appoint an acting Marshal
after the downfall of Nicholas Segrave.

From personal annoyance at Gaveston's behaviour and
the ineptitude of the king, Lancaster and his friends were

[1] The order of the procession is given in *Cal. Cl. R.* (*1307–12*), p. 53. Cf. *Ann.
Paulini* (RS), p. 53.

[2] Of the hereditary Grand Chamberlain (de Vere) nothing is heard in this
reign. The two hereditary chamberlainships of the Exchequer are quite distinct
and had recently been extinguished.

led to attack the administration on wider grounds. Lancaster's appointment as Steward gave him no opening; the only effective way of penetrating into the machinery of household government was through the Marshalship, and here the magnates, since the death of Roger Bigod in 1306, had no opportunity for direct appointment of a deputy who could help them to make trouble. But they could and did arrange that the deputies appointed as acting Marshal in 1308 were chosen from among their own retainers. Thus Clifford, who must be assumed to have 'marshalled' the Wallingford tournament of 1307 and the coronation of 1308, had to take the blame for the anger that was aroused and had to resign. His successor was a Lancastrian retainer, Nicholas Segrave, a well-known baron, named in Lancaster's retinue at the Dunstable tournament in 1309. This is the explanation of the statement in the *Vita Edwardi Secundi* that Lancaster was estranged from the court by the dismissal of one of his men. It is to be noted that Lancaster had no right of appointment to this office: if we did not possess the Dunstable Roll we should not have known that the quarrel was about a retainer, not a deputy.

So the attack broadened out from a personal matter into an attack upon the Marshal's functions. Besides marshalling court functions, with the assistance of the heralds, the marshals of the household had to buy or purvey all the food for the court at the best prices obtainable. This brought the court Marshals into direct touch with the whole population of the countryside through which the court was passing. If the king went to war the business of providing by purveyors was extended on an enormous scale to cover the needs of his troops. How far the king's prerogative right of prise covered purveyances for his army as well as for his household and his castles—for which purveyance was by ancient custom and Magna Carta permissible—had become a great issue between king and barons. It involved the whole right of Prerogative

Taxation if he seized the property of the wool merchants, as he once did, and sold it to pay and feed his troops. The matter had been brought into sudden and urgent prominence by the use of large bodies of infantry in war. In 1297 the number of infantry 'called up' reached 27,000, of whom at least 7,500 were paid for service in the field. Thus Edward I extended an undoubted right of prise (customs duties for Revenue) and fused it with an equally undoubted right of purveyance, but used his right to raise revenue and not merely for household and garrison purposes, but to support the 'war effort' as a whole,[1] claiming *urgens necessitas* as his reason.

One outcome of the crisis in March 1308 had been the banishment of Piers Gaveston to Ireland, not as a private citizen, but as the King's Lieutenant with full powers in proper form.[2] Here he remained, showing considerable ability as a Governor, until the reconciliation with the barons at Stamford on 28 July 1309. This followed close upon the Dunstable tournament, which was no doubt intended, if not to overawe a Parliament, to show that the price of baronial support would be high. The upshot of it was that the status of Piers Gaveston was now much reduced, for part of the price was an obscure renunciation of all the hereditary interests that he had acquired in England, in return, it seems, for a life-interest only, with reversion to the Crown—a common device of the period used conspicuously by Edward I against his magnates. Gaveston's charter of renunciation is maliciously dated 5 August 1309, the second anniversary of his creation as Earl of Cornwall.[3] Before the month was out he received a mandate amounting to a regrant in fee tail for the earldom only, to be held for

---

[1] The inquiry of March 1297 by bannerets in each country into seizure of goods, especially wool and leather, seems to have avoided the use of the word 'purveyance'.   [2] *Parl. Writs*, II, ii, App., p. 15.

[3] *Cal. Cl. R.*, p. 225. G.E.C., *s.v.* Cornwall, alludes to this transaction (*ex* Courthorpe) but gives no reference to the documents in the case. I have not seen it referred to by any other writer, but it is a matter of some interest that seems

three knight's fees 'as in his charter', and at the same time
the reversion of the lands of Bartholomew of Kent in
Halghton in fee tail.[1]

Though purveyances were simply goods taken for the
king, his household, his children, and his castles, at the
royal price, whether or not the army in the field as well as
in garrison be included, the system was open to great
abuse in that payment was made, or rather promised, by
Wardrobe debentures. The seller, that is, was forced to
await the king's convenience for payment, which might
not be forthcoming for years. Hence purveyances on a
large scale could be just as burdensome as prises where
goods were taken for resale, not for consumption.

There was a danger that the king would fuse his traditional right of purveyance, which was part of the prerogative of any feudal lord, with his equally undoubted right
of prise in an emergency. The Statute of Stamford of
1309[2] attempted to clarify the position, and to extend to
purveyance the control that after 1300 the *communitas* had
thought to exercise upon prise. This was part of what
Edward II had to yield for the readmission of Gaveston to
England. But because it was merely part of a wider political
attack on the behaviour of the king and his favourite, it was
soon, although on the Statute book, swallowed up and for-

---

to have been swallowed up and forgotten in the ensuing troubles. From the
Close Roll it is known only that Gaveston resigned all his lands, but Hemingburgh (ii. 275) states that he got them all back for life. Stapleton's Calendar in
Palgrave's *Antient Kalendars and Inventories of the Exchequer* (Record Commission, 1836), i. 51, lists a quit-claim dated 5 August 1309 by Gaveston of all his
lands in England *and Gascony* to the Crown. What seems to be missing is the
regrant for life of the earldom of Cornwall. The whole transaction is parallel to
the equally complicated Bigod surrender and regrant of 1306. Unlike Bigod,
Gaveston had no heirs.

[1] *Foed.* II. i. 86 (28 August 1309).
[2] *Stat. of the Realm*, i. 154, and *Ann. Lond.* (RS), p. 158. The exacerbated
state of grievance in the Stamford parliament is also reflected in a verbose general
complain tabout papal exactions composed in the Chancery and circulated by
a royal messenger to the barons named in it, for sealing by them. The letter
Domus domini is dated 6 August 1309 in *Ann. Lond.* (RS), i. 161–2; cf. *Foed.*
II. i. 84; *CPR*, p. 180,

gotten, in the more ambitious programme of administrative reform announced next year by the Lords Ordainers.

Prises were for revenue. They were standardized and from 1300 were matters for negotiation with the *communitas*. But at the same time purveyances are brought under the heading of prises. *Cap.* 2 of the *Articuli Super Cartas* says that none shall take *Prises* but the King's *Purveyors* or their deputies. It is complained that the king and the servants of his household make great prises where they pass through the realm, without paying, or else much less than the value. The king's takers and purveyors are to take nothing except for his 'household and children' and not for his paid servants. Complaints are to be made to the Steward and Treasurer of the Household, but purveyance could still be made under Privy Seal and continued to be a matter of popular grievance for centuries.

There was in this conflict an attempt on the part of the Crown to extend a right of purveyance into a right of prise, and when this had been foiled an attempt by the opposition to extend to purveyance the limitations successfully applied to prise. The attempt to confuse purveyance and prise resulted in an attempt to impose prerogative taxation where the barons denied that any such right existed. The Statute of Stamford was in effect an attack on the whole machinery of prerogative government as it then existed, but the attempted remedies were insufficient, even when Lancaster was Steward of England and had a banneret to represent his interests in the household.

It had always been the Marshals of the Household and Marshals of the Horse who made purveyances and preparations through the harbingers and buyers, for the passage of the royal caravan or baggage train with its twenty carts of five horses to each cart.[1]

The Dunstable Roll[2] is thought to be a unique record

---

[1] For mid-thirteenth century examples of billeting (livery of the king's marshals) see *CPR* (1252) p. 124, (1255) p. 412, and (1259) p. 57.

[2] The Dunstable Roll used by Dugdale (see the *Baronage*, s.v. Chandos) was printed, but without any serious attempt to control the names, by C. E. Long

of a fully political tournament held at Dunstable in the second year of Edward the son of King Edward, held that is between July 1308 and July 1309. The list contains the names of six earls, each followed by his retinue, and a list following on without a break under the heading *De la Commune*. There is no distinction in status between the personnel of this and any of the other retinues, though they differ in size. As the only surviving tournament roll this is of great interest, even though nothing is known of what took place. But as a tournament it ranks in size and importance with Kenilworth (1279), Nefyn (1284), and Wallingford (2 December 1307), and of these we know even less, except that at Nefyn the concourse was international, and both at Nefyn and Kenilworth ladies were present. But this was a political or even military gathering hostile to the régime, attended by six earls, all of whom were soon to be in arms against the king. So we possess a nominal roll, though without the Heralds and Esquires who must have been there, of the Lancastrian faction in 1309.

Date of the Dunstable Tournament

Mr. F. B. Stitt in an article in the *Antiquaries Journal*, xxxii (1952), 202–3, associates the Dunstable Roll of Arms with a tournament alluded to in a *compotus* roll of the manor of Wymondley (Herts. County Record Office, no. 57523). This roll shows that Sir Giles de Argentine and Sir John de Argentine were provided with fodder at Dunstable for a tournament there at some date before the account closed (apparently on 11 June), probably about the end of March 1309. The top of the roll is decayed and not easily legible in a photograph. The date in the heading of the roll says *usque festum sancti B——* which may be

in *Coll. Top. et Gen.* iv (1837), pp. 61–72, from Brit. Mus. Add. MS. 5848, fols. 145–54, a copy in colours made in December 1776 by the Rev. William Cole from Joseph Holland's sixteenth-century copy in trick, at that time belonging to Mr. Lort. There are ten sixteenth-century copies in trick or blazon. See *CEMRA*, pp. 39–40. In spite of this complicated transmission the instances of uncertain identity are few.

St. Barnabas (11 June), as Mr. Stitt reads it. The roll does not declare itself a View of Account nor does it look like one, but no reason is given for not continuing the account, as would beusual, down to the ensuing Michael-mas.

If the tournament of this account-roll took place before 11 June it is almost certainly not the tournament of the Roll of Arms, unless the writs of prohibition of 14 June—not mentioned by Mr. Stitt—were effective in preventing a *repetition* of a tournament at the end of March. This involves believing in *two* tournaments each concerning the same six earls. It seems more probable that the unique writs of 14 June 1309 addressed to the same six earls who are named on the Dunstable Roll relate to a tournament arranged for, and indeed held, about the end of June. The writs should not be ignored: they can hardly be paralleled in the history of the tournament prior to this date. It is surprising that we hear of no confiscation of estates.

Dunstable was a favourite place for tourneying. There was, for example, one which Maurice de Berkeley, who is not on the roll, attended. It is mentioned in the account rolls at Berkeley Castle cited by Dugdale (*Bar.* i. 355) which show that Maurice tourneyed at Worcester, Dunstable, Stamford, Blyth, and Winchester. No dates are given. Thomas de Berkeley was 'de la Commune' (no. 178) at Dunstable in 1309. By contract with Aymer de Valence dated 2 July 1297 Thomas de Berkeley, banneret, his son Maurice and four other knights, and two esquires for Thomas himself and one each for the four knights and three *valets de mestre* to carry their luggage—a total of twenty-four barbed horses—were bound to serve in peace and war for £50 a year and *bouche à court* and robes (Bain, *Cal. Docs. Scot.* ii. 236. From pp. 250–1, 257 we learn that they had been to Flanders).

Whatever the precise date of this tournament, the *Vita Edwardi* makes it quite clear that such assemblies were only excuses for party meetings or demonstrations. The following table of events will show the connexion between tournaments and politics.

Tournaments held or prohibited in 1309

2 February	At Stamford *or elsewhere* during Lent.[1]
14 April	At Stafford.[2]
18 April	At Newmarket or elsewhere in those parts.[3]
[27 April	Full parliament at Westminster. Gaveston in Ireland.]
12 May	General prohibition, to all sheriffs. Jousts are excepted.[4]
28 May	STEPNEY tournament. Giles de Argentine, King of the Greenwood, jousts against all comers.[5]
12, 14 June	Prohibitions to all sheriffs and five earls individually.[6]
[27 July	The 'hollow reconciliation' at Parliament of prelates and magnates at STAMFORD.]
4 October	General prohibition, to all sheriffs, against tournaments, *or coming armed to Parliament*.[7]

If the Dunstable tournament was held about Easter (as Mr. Stitt believes) any attempt at a repetition of it was checked by the severity of the punishment threatened, and possibly the choice fell upon Stamford as the meeting-place for the July Parliament because it was one of the four recognized tournament-fields in England, by decree of 1194, and could hardly be used for this purpose if Parliament was already there.

The weight of opposition to the Crown thus revealed was due to the growing hatred of Piers Gaveston as a result of his victory in the Wallingford tournament of December 1307, his outrageous behaviour at the Coronation three months later, his marriage into the peerage, his vast estates, his bestowal of pejorative epithets upon the

---

[1] *Cal. Cl. R.*, p. 99 (dated at Guildford).   [2] Ibid., p. 64.
[3] Ibid., p. 110 (dated at Langley).   [4] Ibid., p. 156.
[5] *Ann. Lond.*, p. 159.
[6] *Cal. Cl. R.*, pp. 158–9, dated at Langley. Also in *Parl. Writs* and *Foedera*.
[7] *Cal. Cl. R.*, p. 126.

other earls—all these factors embittered the naturally sullen and factious disposition of Earl Thomas of Lancaster, whose five earldoms gave him an unhealthy territorial preponderance. The opposition to the court crystallized in March 1308 at a Great Council, when the odium for what had happened fell upon Clifford, who was dismissed from his office as acting Marshal, being replaced (12 March–August 1308) by Nicholas Segrave, a Lancastrian retainer at the Dunstable tournament of 1309, and the man whom the *Vita Edwardi* alludes to, but does not name, in mentioning Lancaster's anger at the dismissal of one of his dependants from the court.[1] He was apparently no more popular with the rest of the magnates, as Marshal, than Clifford had been. So the king had no known Marshal at court until the appointment of Thomas de Brotherton in 1315, on the dismissal of Segrave, who is said to have retained the office though he left the court.[2]

Lancaster had already been named Steward of England in 1308,[3] but this gave him no political authority or power to interfere in the royal household, though his supporters were later to make a story about it.

Clifford left the court and appeared next year in the Earl of Warwick's retinue at Dunstable, but he was reappointed as Warden of the Scottish March after the July reconciliation at Stamford, and only lost this office after the Ordainers had come into power.[4] In September 1308 he exercised his functions as hereditary sheriff of Westmorland, but on giving up the Marshalship he left

---

[1] Nicholas Segrave attests a deed of Thomas of Lancaster in 1319, immediately after his Treasurer, Robert de Holland. This document is an indenture granting William Latimer, banneret, land and rent for his services for life in peace and war. Besides about £100 a year in land, Latimer was to receive £1,000 a year for forty men-at-arms in England, Scotland, Ireland, and Wales (15 May 1319 at York). The deed is in G. Holmes, *The Estates of the Higher Nobility in Fourteenth Century England* (Cambridge, 1957), pp. 122–3.

[2] *Ann. Paul.*, p. 264.

[3] *CPR*, p. 68.

[4] *Foed.* ii. 100.

the court, and in this roll he is side by side with Andrew de Harclay ('Herte clawe') of Cumberland.[1] It is perhaps surprising to find that Clifford and Gloucester are clearly aligned with the opposition so early in the reign.

Light is thrown on the Earl of Hereford's retinue at Dunstable by a well-known contract of 1307 between the Earl and Bartholomew de Enfield of Middlesex, who had been knighted at the Feast of the Swans.[2] Bartholomew was to serve in peace and in war, at home and abroad, and in the Holy Land if the earl went there, receiving robes and saddles as his other bachelors, in time of peace hay and oats for four horses, wages for three grooms and his chamberlain dining in hall, in war-time and for 'le turnoi' hay and oats for eight horses, wages for seven grooms and his chamberlain dining in hall, and sufficient equipment for war and the tourney, and he is to receive 40 marks worth of land in Annandale for life. This contract, made at Lochmaben, 15 February 1306/7, illustrates the theme of this chapter, that a tournament of Lancastrian earls is the Lancastrian party on a war-footing.[3] It is also in keeping with the spirit of the age that Earl Thomas, in his treasonable correspondence with the Scots, should be addressed by Sir James Douglas as King Arthur.[4]

The Segraves were barons of Stowe in Northamptonshire. Nicholas Segrave, after a famous quarrel with John de Cromwell in 1305, turned traitor and was imprisoned in Dover castle, where he was allowed to amuse himself in the meadow 'car nous savons bien qe le chevaler nad

[1] When Clifford died in 1314 at Bannockburn, Warwick, Percy, and Badlesmere had themselves made administrators of his property, which seems to point to some arrangement made by Clifford himself in his lifetime. His London house, Clifford's Inn, passed to the Crown on his son's death at Boroughbridge in 1322.

[2] The contract is in Bain, *Cal. Docs. Scot.*, no. 1899. Bartholomew is on PRA, no. 309.

[3] Other important lists of Lancastrian supporters are in *Parl. Writs*, II. ii, App., pp. 66–70 (16 October 1313), being pardons to Earl Thomas and 500 others named for the murder of Gaveston; and again (22 October and 1 November 1318), ibid., pp. 126–32, where the total is over 650.

[4] *Parl. Writs*, II. ii, App., pp. 195–6.

mie talent de senfouyr'.[1] He did escape, but Edward bore
him no malice, and a year later gave him his life.[2] His
eldest brother John, sent by the Marshal as his deputy to
Caerlaverock,[3] had fought at Falkirk, and is of importance
in heraldic history as an example of a deliberate change
of arms. The *Song* says of him:

> Whom nature had adorned
> In body and enriched in heart,
> He had a valiant father
> Who wholly abandoned
> The garbs and assumed the lion,
> And who taught his brave children
> To imitate him and associate with the nobles.

Nicholas used his father's banner *Sable*, with a silver lion
rampant crowned with gold, with a red label on account
of his brother John, who was the eldest. This Nicholas
was the brother of the Warden of Scotland, John Segrave.
On the accession of Edward II he was released from his
obligation to return to prison—the magnates had already
recommended him to mercy—alleging his good service
done and to be done. He then resumed his career in England by becoming Constable of Northampton, a Justice
of the Forest, and in March 1308 Marshal of England
immediately after his pardon in February. It is not known
if Edward II did this because he disliked the man his

---

[1] Pierre Chaplais, 'Some Private Letters of Edward I', in *EHR* (Jan. 1962),
from PRO, Anct. Corr. xii, no. 63.

[2] F. M. Powicke, *The Thirteenth Century* (1953), pp. 331–3.

[3] *Song of Caerlaverock*, p. 5. This Sir John had become the Marshal's retainer in 1297. A detailed agreement was drawn up by which he engaged himself
to serve for the Marshal's life with five bachelors, against all men save the king,
in peace and war in England, Wales, and Scotland, for which he was enfeoffed
with the manor of Loddon in Norfolk. The contract, printed in my *Seignorial
Administration in England*, App. II, pp. 167–8, may be compared with Sir
Philip de Hardreshulle's [Hartshill, co. Warwick] contract with Sir Edmund de
Stafford, a banneret in the Flemish campaign. This deed, dated 3 October 1297
at Ghent, is printed by G. Barraclough, *The Earldom and Palatinate of Chester*
(1953). Edmund is 'Le baroun de Estafforde' in PRA, 144 (see Dugdale,
Baronage, i. 158).

father had appointed, or whether he was trying to please Lancaster. The matter is obscure. Segrave was a Lancastrian retainer, but 'the barons' did not relish his appointment and he was dismissed, as Clifford had been. But he was reinstated: he was driven from the court but did not lose the appointment and continued to 'act' as Marshal for years.[1]

A closer approach to the roll of the Dunstable tournament raises many problems. Its very existence presupposes the presence of heralds. They had to proclaim the tournament and supervise the contestants in action. They were the umpires. There had to be a Marshal for the occasion. A herald drew up this roll, perhaps from lists handed in by the earls and by the *Commune*, led (since he heads the list) by Robert de Tony, the Swan Knight.

The writs of prohibition of 14 June 1309 were directed to the six earls found on the roll, but they do not mention the *Commune*. The earls named, and the strength of their retinues, were as follows:

(1)	Gloucester, nos.	1–22[2]
(2)	Hereford	23–36
(3)	Warwick	37–91
(4)	Lancaster	92–126
(5)	Warenne	127–150
(6)	Arundel	151–164
(7)	*De la Commune*	165 (Robert de Tony)–235

Of these earls, Hereford, Warenne, and Arundel had been defeated by Gaveston at Wallingford on 2 December 1307.

The *Commune* appears to be largely an assembly of 70 unattached knights, men not in the retinues of great lords, but simple knights who could not afford to embody a troop. Yet it may have been subdivided, for it includes half a dozen barons by tenure who appear as bannerets in

[1] See Conway Davies, Index, s.v. Segrave.
[2] There are no writs to Cornwall, Richmond, Pembroke, or Lincoln, and they were not summoned by writ to Parliament at Stamford either, as being, perhaps, already with the court.

the PRA. It is led by a well-known banneret, Robert de Tony, the Swan Knight of the Caerlaverock poem, who had been a banneret in the Flanders campaign in 1297. He died a few months after the tournament, in September 1309. But by and large this is a list of bachelors. That it includes barons by tenure means nothing. The idea seems to have gained currency among some writers that a baron was a presumptive banneret, but this is not so.[1] Six of these barons are here, but they may be fighting, like Brian FitzAlan and later Chandos, as bachelors.[2] This I suspect to be the truth.[3]

These men, if they ever took the field in 1309 with their esquires and sergeants, would have made up a formidable army, and if they tourneyed it would have been a remarkable business if they had gone beyond jousting. It looks much more like a political tournament, almost a Lancastrian parliament, or a dress rehearsal for one. Some of the tournament men are in fact recognizable as honourable and gallant members at the Easter Parliament.

From the military point of view this is the earliest known list of the Lancastrian party on a war footing. It is also the only known list of persons present at a tournament in England up to this time. But we know nothing of what actually happened. If the *Commune* is not simply a list of unattached knights bachelor, what else do they have in common, and why are they grouped apart? Above all, who fought against whom?

Perhaps the tournament of Dunstable is best regarded as a cloak for political discussion, and an overt threat to the established government of the country, an attempt to overawe the king and strike fear into the heart of Gaveston

---

[1] e.g. Morris, *Welsh Wars*. See p. 23, *supra*.

[2] Pecché is no. 167 = PRA 88, the brothers Hastings nos. 180–1 = PRA 21–22, Maltravers no. 191 = PRA 148, Courtenay no. 196 = PRA 45, Camoys no. 208 = PRA 160.

[3] Dare we regard the *Communitas Bachelerie* of 1259 as the unattached bachelors, *not* the retainers? In 1259 even more than in 1309 we should expect to find many knights not yet absorbed into the magnate–retainer relationship.

L

whom they had had reason to hate and fear in their turn in a more conventional encounter. However this may be, the roll remains, to suggest, with other Rolls of Arms, some valuable conclusions in the realm of social history.

The fifteen knights at the Dunstable tournament who are also found as M.P.s are as follows:

			Kt. of Shire for
At the Parliament of Westminster, May 1306			
Ralph de Friskeneye	Lanc. retainer		Lincoln
At the Parliament of Carlisle, January 1307			
Simon de Mamecestre	*de la Commune*[1]	(PRA 843 War.)	Warwick[2]
John de Somery	,,	(PRA 408)	Hertford
William Marmion	,,		Leicester
Ralph de Friskeney	Lanc. retainer		Lincoln
Fulk Payforer	Glouc. ,,	(PRA 283 Kent)	Kent[3]
William le Blunt	Warwick ,,	(PRA 837)	
Walter Haket	*de la Commune*	(PRA 630 D. & N.)	Worcs.
At Northampton, October 1307			
William Marmion	*de la Commune*		Leicester
Roland de Coykin	Warw. retainer	(PRA 178)	Cornwall
Laurence de Hameldone	Glouc. ,,	(PRA 527 Suff.)	Somerset
At Westminster, April 1309			
William Creye	*de la Commune*	(PRA 286)	Kent
John of Elsefield	Glouc. retainer		Oxon.
John Lestrange de Erkalewe	Arundel ,,	(? PRA 70)	Salop.
John de Scures	Arundel ,,		Hants
John D'Abernon	*de la Commune*		Surrey and Sussex[4]

[1] The elaborate note on *Communitas* in the French edition of Stubbs's *Constitutional History* (ed. C. Petit-Dutaillis), iii. 851, does not help towards an explanation of the *Commune* at Dunstable, though in 1343 the phrase *des chivalers des countez et autres communes* may be noted.

[2] And 30 May 1306.

[3] And again Oct. 1307.

[4] And in Parliaments of 6 Oct. 1297, 25 May 1298, but this may be the father.

X

KNIGHTS OF THE SHIRE AND SHERIFFS

HERALDIC evidence is of considerable use in assess-
ing the social standing of Edwardian members of
parliament and royal officials. The question is
tedious to attack in detail, but the answers are easily
available from the evidence of the combined Rolls of
Arms used in this book. It is unnecessary to look for
political or providential reasons in the fusion of knights
and burgesses into one house, because the richer burgesses
usually held land outside their towns, the knights of the
shire were even *temp.* Ed. I & II often not (so far as we
know) gentlemen of coat-armour, and as Stubbs remarked,
the younger sons of the country knights sought 'wife, occupation, and estate' in the towns.[1]

The use of heraldry in this connexion is not merely
to single out persons of original or achieved gentility, but
within a chosen term of years to distinguish members of a
military class from those who were not 'strenuous knights'.
Indeed, the growing use of that adjective by chroniclers
shows that knighthood, even *c.* 1300, did not always imply
military skill or activity. In the king's household to be a
king's banneret is the highest rank available for a clerk,
unless he is to become a bishop. Thus judges can be made
bannerets.

---

[1] Stubbs, *Constitutional History*, xv. 196–7. It is, however, always to be remembered that the knights themselves in Parliament were paid as bannerets,
while the burgesses were paid at the same rate as knights bachelor. The knights
may have led the burgesses, but it may be doubted if they talked more. An
estate of burgesses meeting apart as merchants at a *Colloquium* at York, where on
25 July 1303 forty-two towns were represented, was far from submissive.

Much has been written about the administrative functions of the medieval sheriff, and the personnel of 'the Commons' has been analysed in regard to their other administrative functions and their attendance at Parliament.[1] But for the period 1272–1310 not much has been said about the social status of these men, how far the categories of knights of the shire and sheriff overlapped, or how many of the M.P.s were active knights and how many professional administrators. This is particularly true of the reign of Edward I: the reign of Edward II has received more attention.[2] The period 1258–67 is also being thoroughly investigated, a period when knights are needed for Grand Juries, the collection of taxes, to act as coroners or forest officials, or as stewards and constables to the king or private lords.[3]

There is insufficient heraldic evidence in the Rolls of Arms for an assessment in this way of the social position of the sheriffs or knights of the shire before 1295.[4] The unique powers concentrated in the hands of the Lord Edward during the years 1266–74 had included the right of nominating, by himself or through Roger Mortimer, the Archbishop of York, or Earl Richard of Cornwall, almost all the sheriffs. When full heraldic information

[1] The bibliography of the history of Parliament in this period is best approached through the 1961 edition of the *Handbook of British Chronology*, ed. Sir F. M. Powicke and E. B. Fryde, pp. 492 ff.

[2] G. Lapsley, 'Knights of the Shire in the Parliaments of Edward II', in *EHR* (1914), deals only with Camb., Hunts., Beds., Herts., and Essex, and only with the political 'high-spots' of the reign. The Parliament of 1307 is given, but those through 1308 and up to 1311 are neglected.

Professor J. G. (now Sir Goronwy) Edwards published a statistical investigation into 'The Personnel of the Commons' in *Essays presented to T. F. Tout* (1925); see p. 205 for the parliamentary career of Gerard de Braybrooke in Bucks., Herts., and Beds.

[3] R. F. Treharne, 'The Baronial Reform Movement', in *T. R. Hist. S.* (1943), and 'The Knights in the Period of Rebellion and Reform' in *BIHR* (1948). But the escheators should not, for the Edwardian period, be numbered among the knights.

[4] In an important review of Professor W. A. Morris's book on *The Sheriff*, Miss Cam pointed out that Professor Morris had omitted to deal with the social standing of the sheriff in the thirteenth century.

does come to hand it is found for the years 1295–1309 that there were at least 163 armigerous M.P.s—some re-elected many times for the same or different counties, and some 200 non-armigerous M.P.s. This is to say that 102 of the strenuous knights served also as knights of the shire at one time or another. What is more important is that so large a number of M.P.s should not even at this early date be gentlemen of coat-armour. But the combined totals of our Rolls of Arms cannot be claimed as a complete picture, so that the weight allowed to this result must remain a matter of opinion.

From 1327, and possibly earlier, the customary rates of pay were 4s. a day for knights and 2s. a day for burgesses.[1] The county members, that is, received preferential treatment as bannerets, while the burgesses were paid as bachelors. Miss McKisack has pointed out that by the fifteenth century the smaller boroughs elected knights and esquires who were neither resident nor even burgesses and that re-election was just as common in the boroughs as in the shires.[2]

This brief glance at the composition of the estate of the Commons, in which from the earliest times for which records are available many of the 'knights' are not armigerous and probably have not even been dubbed, leads to the observation that the 'strenuous' or armigerous knights are not coextensive as a class with the country gentry. The unwarlike members of this class outnumbered their more warlike neighbours by at least two to one. Most of these men, too, could in our period be named, because if they were rich enough, or were thought by the government to be rich enough, to be knights they were subject, or could be subject, to 'distraint of knighthood'. They could and did serve as M.P.s or escheators—but rarely as sheriffs—and we suspect that many of them were farmers of their

---

[1] M. McKisack, *Borough Representation*, pp. 82, 100. The rate was fixed under Edward II by the writ *de expensis levandis* (Tuswell-Langmeed, ed. Plucknett, p. 646). [2] Op. cit., pp. 22, 110.

own lands. Often, as younger sons, they became monks or friars or beneficed clergy, but in any case they fall outside the scope of this book.

By far the greater number of sheriffs between 1254 and 1309 were gentlemen of coat-armour, but their social status differed much according to the county in which they served. It is a remarkable feature of the social and political history of the knightage in England that even over a period of thirty years or so the names of the families concerned quite change. The turnover in family names is so great that in research over an extended period it is difficult to assess the results—if the researcher lives long enough to arrive at any. Similar changes in the high ranks of society are often concealed by the continuity of titles.

(I) KNIGHTS OF THE SHIRE

It is possible to know almost anything about the thirteenth-century knights of the shire except what they said and did in Parliament. Their often-quoted reluctance to serve is not borne out by the facts. Professor Jacob has shrewdly remarked of the fifteenth century 'the old dislike of attendance at parliaments, if indeed it ever existed, has passed away. Election extended now beyond the *milites gladio cincti* to the general run of country gentry and lawyers and business men, administrators, were not avoided.'[1] In an earlier generation there had been a feeling among the magnates that if they did not agree personally to an aid at Westminster they ought not to pay it, and this feeling extended to the boroughs, continuing to a later date. But it existed for a different reason. If a borough sent members to parliament it would be taxed, and the boroughs paid at a higher rate than the communities of the shires. Hence it was in their interest to be unrepresented and taxed with the county. It is the taxation, not the representation, that is unpopular.

[1] E. F. Jacob, *The Fifteenth Century*, pp. 408–9.

Instances are numerous of knights being elected for the same county over a period of many years. This is so common that being an M.P. is for some knights almost a profession. It was common also for a knight to be elected for one county this year and another the next. He could be elected for a shire in which the bulk of his property (as indicated in the PRA) did not lie.

John de Aungervile was elected six times for Leicestershire.

John Ayngnel twice for Herefordshire and four times for Herts. (1298–1309).

Baldwin de Bello Alneto six times for Hants.

Reginald de Boville seven times for Cornwall.

Thomas de Burnham five or six times for Lincs.

Hugh de Estcote six times for Hants.

Ralph Paynel for Lincolnshire in 1297 and 1308.

Sometimes the knights of the shire wandered but not, I think, often. *Gerard de Braybrok*, a Buckinghamshire knight (PRA, 370), was returned for Bedfordshire in 1301, Bucks. in 1309, and Hertfordshire twice in 1307.

A special case of re-election occurred when the knights who had been sent to York in 1298 were ordered to be sent to Lincoln in 1301 because they were to receive the reports of the Perambulators of the Forest appointed at York.

Some of the knights of the shire were 'strenuous knights', gentlemen of coat-armour. Amongst the persons receiving military summonses to be at York on 25 May 1298 for an expedition against the Scots we find

Hugh le Blount who is returned for Essex the same day.

John D'Abernon for Surrey.

Peter Dammartin for Suffolk.

Jollan de Duresme for Essex.

Henry de Enfield for Middlesex (military summons for Essex).

John fitz Guy for Warwick (military summons for Oxon.).

Henry Mauveysin for Staffs.

Ralph Saunzaver for Sussex.

Eight of the knights of the shire, that is, were ordered to report for military service at York on the day that they were to be in Parliament there.

Eleven of the knights on the Dunstable Tournament Roll (1309) were county members of Parliament between 1295 and 1307. Five of them were present in April 1309 at Westminster. At the Stamford parliament in July 1309 there were no knights.

An oddity that does not seem to have been noticed is that instances are found where a man has been elected twice, that is by two separate shires—and shires under different sheriffs—to the same Parliament. These are:

> Hugh le Blount, Berks. and Essex, 1300.
> Richard of Windsor, Berks. and Middlesex, Oct. 1297.
> John of Acton, Gloucester and Hereford, 1301.
> John de la Poile, Middlesex and Surrey, Oct. 1307.

Some knights were foreigners in the county for which they were elected. James de Norton, who was knighted by the king at Christmas 1305 at Kingston Lacy in Dorset, had his livery of the king (by writ of Privy Seal dated 23 November) and was a few months later returned to the Whitsuntide Parliament as knight of the shire for Hampshire. I do not know if he was admitted as a King's Bachelor. He was a Worcester and Hereford man who bore a gold lion on a green shield (*de vert a un lion de or*, PRA, 233).

(II) SHERIFFS

In the middle of the thirteenth century the appointment of sheriffs had been regarded as a vital matter, and a great point of dispute between king and baronage. In the course of the next fifty years this feeling quite disappeared. Under the Lord Edward, while he was away on Crusade, his nominees tended to be of baronial rank, but the general tendency is for the sheriff to become more and more

professional and less of a great man—two *magistri* appear
—and it is not infrequent, as the following list shows, for
a man to serve as sheriff in different counties at different
times. Their tenure of office was not often prolonged under Edward I. The work, with the enormous enlargement
of the number and variety of writs to be returned, was
highly specialized and the rewards of office were closely
watched by the crown.

Perhaps it happened that when these men had made
themselves known at Westminster as representing their
shires, they were sent back as sheriffs. For whatever reason,
it happens increasingly between 1260 and 1310 that the
sheriff becomes a member of Parliament. The office of
sheriff was declining, with the loss of military functions to
Commissioners of Array, and judicial powers to special
commissions (such as Trailbaston, from 1306). So the
problem of choosing sheriffs became less urgent and when,
having ceased to be disputed between king and barons,
the privilege of choosing their own sheriffs was granted
to the counties themselves (in 1300), they sometimes
elected the men already in office. It was frequent to elect
a man who had been sheriff in the county concerned or in
another. Occasionally the serving sheriff was returned as
M.P. There was indeed in many counties little choice if
strenuus or even administratively active knights were to be
sent.

Sheriffs

Dene, John de	War. & Leics.	1302
		1305 (Apr.)
	Salop. & Staffs.	1305 (Oct.)
		1307
	War. & Leics.	1307, 1310
Gardino, Thomas de	Gloucester	1293–8
PRA, 607		1302–7
	Camb. & Hunt.	1298–(1300?)
Gerberge, Mr. John	Som. & Dorset	1297
	Hants.	1301

Hereward, Robert, PRA, 599	Camb. & Hunt.	1300–1
	Norf. & Suff.	1301–6
Hevre [Hever], William de	Kent	20 Mar. 1272 & Oct. 1274
	Surrey & Sussex	1274–5
Lee, John de la	Somerset & Dorset	1301
	Hampshire	1302
	Essex & Herts.	1299, 1304
Seyton, Mr. Roger de	Northants.	1272
Shelfhanger, Walter de	Lincs.	1273–4
	Camb. & Hunt.	1274–5
	Norf. & Suff.	1275–7
Styrcheslegh, Walter de	Wilts.	1272
	Notts. & Derby	1274–8
	Gloucs.	1280–2
	Lincs.	1282–5

Sheriffs (S) who *also served as Knights* (K) *of the Shire*

(A) Armigerous sheriffs and *M.P.s.*

(B) *Not* known to be armigerous, from PRA, 'Swan Knights', Caerlaverock, Dering, and Falkirk Rolls, nor in 'Three 13th cent. Rolls of Arms' as printed in *Archaeologia*, vol. 39, nor in Collins.

[This list does not include those who were merely re-elected as *Knights* or reappointed as *Sheriffs*.]

(B) *Acton*, John de, (S) *Hereford*, 10 Dec. 1294–1 Oct. 1299, April–November 1303, *Salop & Staffs.*, Feb. 1304–1 Oct. 1305; (K) *Hereford*, 6 Mar. 1300, 20 Jan. 1301, *Gloucester*, 20 Jan. 1301.

(B) *Annesleye*, John de, (S) *Notts.*, 11 Nov. 1285–1290; (K) *Notts.*, 27 Nov. 1285.

(B) *Apeldrefeld*, Henry de, (S) *Kent*, 21 Apr. 1298–1 Oct. 1299; (K) *Kent*, 20 Jan. 1301, 16 Feb. 1305.

(B) *Bastenthwueit*, Alexander de, (S) *Cumb.*, 28 Mar. 1307; (K) *Cumb.*, 13 Oct. 1307, 27 Apr. 1309.

(A) *Bathonia*, Nicholas de, (K) *Gloucs.*, Jan. 1307 (St. George's Roll 448).

(B) *Beysin* (Beysey, Bessy), Walter de, (K) *Salop*, 29 Sept. 1302; (S) *Salop & Staffs.*, 1303.

(A) *Bigod*, Ralph le, (K) *Essex*, 30 May 1306 (St. George's Roll 301).

(A) *Botiler*, Henry le, (K) *Lancs.*

(B) *Bradenham*, Simon de, (K) *Camb.*, 27 Nov. 1295; (S) *Beds. & Bucks.*, 1296–7, *Essex & Herts.*, 28 Oct. 1297.

(B) *Broughton*, John de, (K) *Hunt.*, 16 Feb. 1305; (S) *War. & Leics.*, 5 May 1298–(?18 Oct. 1300).

(A) *Bruyll* (Bruly), Henry de, (K) *Oxon.*, 1297, 1298 (St. George's Roll 643).

(A) *Burghulle*, Roger de, (K) *Heref.*, 27 Nov. 1295; (S) *Heref.*, 1278–(?1291) (St. George's Roll 669).

(B) *Burghunte*, Richard de, (K) *Hants*, 20 Jan. 1307; (S) *Som. & Dorset*, 25 Oct. 1289–13 May 1291.

(B) *Cambhou*, John de, (K) *Northumb.*, 1301, 1302, 1304/5; (S) 1301–3.

(B) *Chaddeworth*, William de, (K) *Notts.*, 6 Mar. 1300; (S) *Notts. & Derby*, 1290–1.

(B) *Coleshill*, Richard de, (K) *Berks.*, 1295; (S) *Dorset & Som.*, 2 Nov. 1274–? 25 Oct. 1278.

(B) *Corbet*, Ralph, (K) *Salop*, 1290, 1295; (S) *Salop & Staffs.*, 1288–9.

(A) *Crok*, Peter, (K) *Gloucs.*, 1302 (St. George's Roll 566).

(A) *Croupes*, Richard de, (K) *Gloucs.*, 1301 (St. George's Roll 634, cf. 482).

(A) *Crumbe*, Simon de, (K) *Worcs.*, 1295, 1299, 1301 (St. George's Roll 595).

(B) *Dene*, John de, (K) *Hunts.*, 1300; (S) *War. & Leics.*, 1302, *Salop & Staffs.*, 1 Oct. 1305–11 Nov. 1307.

(A) *Dowmore* (*Donmer*), John de, (K) *Som.*, May 1306 (St. George's Roll 582).

(A) *Elmerig* (or *Elmebrig*), Adam de, (K) *Worcs.* (St. George's Roll 269).

(A) *Estcote*, Hugh de, (K) *Hants*, six times, 1297–1305 (St. George's Roll 452).

(A) *Etchingham*, William de, (K) *Sussex*, 16 Feb. 1305 (Soc. of Antiq. 112).

(A) *Fitz Eustace*, Thomas, (K) *Linc.*, 6 Oct. 1251; (S) 1303–5, PRA 658.

(A) *Folejaumbe*, Thomas, (K) *Derby*, four times, 1297–1309 (St. George's Roll 580).

(B) *Furneus*, Richard de, (K) *Notts.*, 25 May 1298; (S) *Notts. & Derby*, 1300–1.

(B) *Gedding*, Walter de, (K) *Surrey*, 20 May 1300; (S) *Surrey & Sussex*, 1303–4.

(B) *Grapinel*, Henry, (K) *Essex*, 6 Oct. 1297; (S) *Essex*, 1290.

(A) *Gresleye*, Geoffrey de, (K) *Derby*, 1300, 1301 (St. George's Roll 451, Soc. of Antiq. 345).

(A) *Gubium* [*Gobyon*], Hugh, (K) *Northumb.*, 1302; (S) 1292–6, PRA 739.

(A) *Hamelyn*, William, (K) *Leics.*, 1290; (S) *War. & Leics.*, 1275–8 (Collins 488).

(A) *Harlee*, Richard, (K) *Salop & Staffs.*, four times, 1301–7; (S) *Salop & Staffs.*, 1301–3 [445 *Soc. of Antiq. Roll* 105], PRA 973 (*Harlee*).

(A) *Haveringes*, Richard de, (K) *Dorset*, 30 May 1306 (St. George's Roll 660).

(A) *Helyon*, Walter de, (K) *Gloucs.*, 1295 (St. George's Roll 514) (Soc. of Antiq. 252).

(A) *Hoo*, Robert de, (K) *Camb.*, 30 May 1306; (S) *Camb.*, 1306 (St. George's Roll).

(A) *Hopton*, Walter de, (K) *Heref.*, 1305 (St. George's Roll 276, Soc. of Antiq. 257).

(B) *Huwell*, Richard de, (K) *Linc.*, 1297; (S) *Linc.*, 1299–1300.

(A) *Kirkham*, Nicholas de, (K) *Devon*, 1301 (St. George's Roll 564 = Antiq. 145).

(B) *Langley*, John de, (K) *Gloucs.*, 1298; (S) *Gloucs.*, 1298–9, 1307– .

(A) *Lillebonne*, William de, (K) *Wilts.*, 1306 (St. George's Roll 271 = Antiq. 432).

(A) *De la Mare*, John, (K) *Heref.*, 1298 (St. George's Roll 579).

(B) *Mulcastre*, William de, (K) *Cumb.*, April 1309; (S) *Cumb.*, 1298.

(A) *Multon*, Hubert de, (K) *Cumb.*, 1295 (*St. George's Roll* 348, 326).

(B) *Nouwers*, Almaric de, (K) *Bucks.*, 1297; (S) *Northants.*, 1307.

(A) *Pichard*, Miles, *Kgs. kt.*, (K) *Heref.*, 1302, 1307; (S) *Heref.* 1299–1305 (with deputy while serving in Scotland).

(B) *Rabaz*, Stephen, (K) *Northants.*, May 1298; (S) *War. & Leics.* 1290–(?1293).

(B) *Roshale*, Thomas de, (K) *Salop*, 1300, 1301, 1302; (S) *Heref.*, 1306–7.

(B) *St. Omer*, Thomas de, (K) *Wilts.*, 1305; (S) *Norf. & Suff.*, 1307.

(A) *Scirlee* (Sch-), Ralph de, (K) *War.*, 1295; (S) *Salop*, 1295–8, *Notts. & Derby*, 1298–1300, *Salop*, 1301–3, PRA 859.

(A) *Seneschal*, *William le*, (K) *Worcs.*, 1295, 1297, 1298 (St. George's Roll 577).

(B) *Seyton*, John de, (K) *Rutl.*, 1302, *Northants.*, 1305; (S) *Northants.*, 1302–3.

(A) *Springhos*, Roger, (K) *Salop*, 1295; (S) *Salop & Staffs.*, 1278–86 (St. George's Roll 388 = Antiq. 251).

(B) *Tailboys* (Taleboys), Lucas, (K) *Northumb.*, 1300; (S) *Northumb.*, 1303–4.

(B) *Trouewyne* (Trom or Trumwyne), William, (K) *Staffs.*, 1302, 1305; (S) 1307.

(B) *Valoniis*, Warresius de, (K) *Kent*, 1301, 1302, 1306; (S) *Kent*, 1303–4.

(A) *Vaux* (Vallibus), John de, (K) *Northumb.*, 1306 (St. George's Roll 240).

(B) *Ver*, Robert de, (K) *Northants.*, 1306; (S) *Northants.*, 1301–2.

(A) *Warbleton*, Thomas de, (K) *Hants*, 1307; (S) *Hants*, 1297–1301, 1303–5, 1306 (St. George's Roll 245 = Soc. of Antiq. 360).

(B) *Wodeton*, Robert de, (K) *Devon*, 1295; (S) *Devon*, 1285.

Our results can to some extent be general, but there are certain limiting factors. The heraldic evidence is much fuller for the border counties and for the south coast, because the marches naturally show a higher percentage of strenuous knights than the midland counties.

The second difficulty is that so many knightly families prominent in 1270 are no longer so in 1320. The change of names from generation to generation makes it difficult to make broad comparisons even within the limits of a single county. Anyone who has worked over a series of local charters with their lists of witnesses will be aware of this feature of English social history.

We are, however, dealing only with about a third of the country gentry. The rest were not gentlemen of coat-armour. If a man advertised himself in this period by using a coat of arms it meant that he was prepared to fight. But there were a great many peace-loving folk at all times who were prepared to forgo this privilege by evasion or to buy themselves out, and the number of knights in the country grew even more restricted in the later middle ages.

Even within the chivalrous class there was a subsection of busybodies, professional knights who are active to the point of ubiquity. These men appear as knights of the shire, and as sheriffs, with surprising frequency.

The country gentry were the class who, until the late nineteenth century, performed the whole work of local government in England. But like any other section of English society in any age this class had no exact or fixed bounds. It shades off into the nobility at one end of the scale and the yeomanry or troopers at the other. There is also a growth of literacy among knights that enables the government to extend their usefulness, and on the other hand the growing professionalism in the arts of administration that leads to the rise of great clerks who are rewarded with knighthoods within the royal household, or as judges, and are not ordained as priests. Much of the king's business in the shires is conducted, if it relates to the royal demesne or to land held in chief from the crown, by the Escheators. They had no military or judicial functions, but they had 'inquests' and their 'courts' kept records, and it was this superficial similarity to the functions of the Coroner, possibly, that enabled them to practise the kind of fraud that is glanced at in Article XI of the Statute of Stamford (July 1309), by pretending to hold 'courts' and ousting men without lawful trial from lands held in chief. But these escheators were clerks, not knights. Two of them are quite widely known, Mr. Henry de Bray from his estate-book, and Mr. John Walwayn, who became Treasurer of England in 1318. The *Inquisitiones post mortem* show that they must have been full of good stories, and seem to have been recruited from the country gentry, whose younger sons may have provided the bulk of the very numerous king's clerks.

LIST OF WORKS CITED

BAIN, JOSEPH, 'Sir Alexander Balliol', in *The Genealogist* (NS), iv (1880), 141–3.

—— *Calendar of Documents Relating to Scotland*, vol. ii (Edinburgh, 1884).

BARRACLOUGH, GEOFFREY, *The Earldom and Palatinate of Chester* (1953).

BARRON, E. M., *The Scottish War of Independence* (1914).

BÉMONT, C., ed. JACOB, E. F., *Simon de Montfort* (Oxford, 1930).

BOTFIELD, BERIAH, *Manners and Household Expenses* (Roxburghe Club, 1841).

CAM, HELEN, 'The Decline and Fall of English Feudalism', in *History* (December, 1940), pp. 216–33.

CAMPBELL, ALEXANDER, *The History of Dover Castle*, ed. William Darell (1786–97).

CHAMBERS, E. K., *The Mediaeval Stage* (1903).

—— R. W., 'The Continuity of English Prose', in *Thomas More* (E.E.T.S., 1935).

CHAPLAIS, PIERRE, 'Some Private Letters of Edward I', in *EHR* (January 1962).

CLOWES, Sir WILLIAM LAIRD, *History of the Royal Navy* (London, 1897–1903).

COULTON, G. G., *Medieval Panorama* (Cambridge, 1947).

DAVIES, CONWAY, *The Baronial Opposition to Edward II* (Manchester, 1918).

DENHOLM-YOUNG, N., *Richard of Cornwall* (Blackwell, 1947).

—— 'The Tournament in the Thirteenth Century', in *Essays Presented to F. M. Powicke* (Oxford, 1948).

—— *Handwriting in England and Wales* (Cardiff, 1954).

—— *Vita Edwardi Secundi* (Nelson's Med. Latin Classics, 1957).

—— 'The Authorship of the *Vita Edwardi Secundi*', in *EHR* (1956).

—— *Seignorial Administration in England* (Oxford, *reissued* 1963).

—— 'The Song of Caerlaverock and the Parliamentary Roll of Arms', in *Proc. Brit. Acad.* (1962).

DUGDALE, Sir WILLIAM, *The Baronage of England* (1675).

EDWARDS, J. G., 'The Treason of Thomas Turberville', in *Essays Presented to F. M. Powicke* (Oxford, 1948), pp. 269–309.

—— 'The Personnel of the House of Commons', in *Essays Presented to T. F. Tout* (Manchester, 1925).

—— *Littere Wallie* (Cardiff, 1940).

EYTON, R. W., *Shropshire*, 12 vols. (London, 1854–60).

FARRER, WILLIAM, *Honours and Knight's Fees*, vols. i–iii (1923–5).

Fleta, ed. J. SELDEN, 2nd ed., London, 1685.

GALBRAITH, V. H., 'The Literacy of Medieval English Kings', being the Raleigh Lecture to the British Academy (10 July 1935).

GOODMAN, A. W., *Chartulary of Winchester Cathedral* (1926).

GOUGH, HENRY, *Scotland in 1298* (Edinburgh, 1888).

GREENSTREET, JAMES, 'The Nativity Roll', in *The Reliquary*, xv (1875), 27–32, 68–74.

—— The Heralds' Roll, edited as Planché's Roll, in *The Genealogist*, iii (1886), 148–55, 240–4; iv (1887), 17–22, 197–203; v (1888), 173–9.

HALL, HUBERT, *The Red Book of the Exchequer* (RS), 3 vols., 1896.

HARCOURT, L. W. VERNON, *His Grace the Steward and Trial by Peers* (London, 1907).

HARDING, ALAN, 'The Origins and Early History of the Keepers of the Peace', in *T. R. Hist. Soc.* (1960), pp. 85–109.

HASSALL, A. G. and W. O., *The Douce Apocalypse* (Faber & Faber, 1962).

HEMINGBURGH, WALTER, *Chronicle*, ed. H. Rothwell for Camden Soc. (1957).

HOLLISTER, C. WARREN, 'The Significance of Scutage Rates in Eleventh- and Twelfth-Century England', in *EHR*, lxxv (October 1960).

HOLMES, G., *The Estates of the Higher Nobility in the Fourteenth Century* (Cambridge, 1957).

HOMANS, G. C., *The English Villagers of the Thirteenth Century* (Harvard University Press, 1941).

HOWELL, MARGARET, *Regalian Right in Medieval England* (London, 1962).

JACOB, E. F., *The Fifteenth Century* (Oxford, 1961).

JOHNSON, CHARLES, *Dialogus de Scaccario* (Nelson, 1950).

JOHNSTONE, HILDA, *Edward of Caernarvon* (1946).

JOHNSTONE, HILDA, 'The Wardrobe and Household of the Sons of Edward I', in *BIHR*, vol. ii, no. 5.

KANTOROWICZ, ERNST, 'Inalienability', in *Speculum* (1954).

KEEN, M. H., 'Treason Trials under the Law of Arms', in *T. R. Hist. Soc.* (1962), pp. 85–103.

KENDRICK, T. D., *British Antiquity* (London, 1950).

KER, N. R., 'The date of the "Tremulous" Worcester Hand', in *Leeds Studies in English and Kindred Languages* (1937), pp. 28–29.

KITCHIN, G. W., *Obedientary Rolls of St. Swithun's, Winchester* (Hants Rec. Soc., 1892).

LAPSLEY, GAILLARD, 'Knights of the Shire in the Parliaments of Edward II', in *EHR* (1914).

—— 'Buzones', in *EHR* (1947), pp. 177–193, 545–67.

LAVISSE, E., *Histoire de France* (Paris, 1901), vol. iii.

LEES, BEATRICE A., 'Villa Integra', in *EHR*, lxiii (1948), 528–33.

LEWIS, ALAN, 'Roger Leyburne and the Pacification of England, 1265–1267', in *EHR*, liv (1939), 193–214.

Liber Quotidianus Contrarotulatoris Garderobe, 28 Ed. I (Soc. of Antiquaries, 1787).

LONG, C. E., [the Dunstable Roll] in *Coll. Top. et Gen.* iv (1837), 61–72.

LOOMIS, R. S., 'Edward I, Arthurian Enthusiast', in *Speculum*, xxviii (1953), pp. 114–27.

LOWE, E. A., JACOB, E. F., and JAMES, M. R., *Illustrations to the Life of St. Alban* (Roxburghe Club, 1924).

LOYD, LEWIS C., and STENTON, DORIS MARY, *Sir Christopher Hatton's 'Book of Seals'*, Northamptonshire Record Society, no. 94 (1950).

LYON, BRUCE D., 'The Money Fief under the English Kings', in *EHR*, lxvi (1951).

McKISACK, M., *The Parliamentary Representation of the English Boroughs during the Middle Ages* (Oxford, 1932).

MADOX, T., *History of the Exchequer*, ed. 1711.

MAWER, A., and STENTON, F. M., with E. B. GOVER, *Place Names of Sussex*, Part II (1930).

MEEKINGS, C. A. F., 'Adam Fitzwilliam', *BIHR* (May 1961), pp. 1–15.

MEYER, PAUL, ed., *Histoire de Guillaume le Maréchal*, 3 vols. (Soc. de l'Hist. de France, 1891–1901).

MICHEL, F., ed., *Histoire des Ducs* (Paris, 1857).

MORRIS, J. E., *The Welsh Wars of Edward I* (Oxford, 1901).

MORRIS, W. A., *The Medieval English Sheriff to 1300* (Manchester, 1927).

NICHOLS, F. M., 'On Feudal and Obligatory Knighthood', in *Archaeologia*, vol. 39 (1863), pp. 189–244.

NICOLAS, Sir HARRIS, *History of the Royal Navy*, vol. i (1847).

PAINTER, S., *William the Marshal* (Baltimore, 1933).

—— 'Castle-Guard', in *American Historical Review*, xl (1935), 450–9.

PALGRAVE, F., *Antient Kalendars and Inventories of the Exchequer* (1836).

PECHAM'S *Registrum: Registrum epistolarum Fratris Johannis de Peckham*, ed. C. T. MARTIN, 3 vols. (RS, 1882–5).

PICKFORD, C. E., 'The Three Crowns of King Arthur', in *Yorkshire Archaeological Journal*, xxxviii (1954).

POOLE, A. L., *From Domesday Book to Magna Carta* (Oxford, 1951).

POWICKE, Sir F. M., *The Thirteenth Century, 1216–1307* (Oxford, 1954).

—— 'Loretta, Countess of Leicester', in *Historical Essays in Honour of James Tait* (Manchester, 1933).

—— and FRYDE, E. B., *Handbook of British Chronology* (1961).

RAMSAY, Sir J. H., *The Dawn of the Constitution* (1908).

REID, Miss R., 'Barony and Thanage', in *EHR*, xxxii (1917).

RICHARDSON, H. G., 'The English Coronation Oath', in *Speculum*, xxiv (1949), 44–75.

ROUND, J. H., *Peerage and Pedigree* (1910).

—— *The King's Sergeants and Officers of State with Their Coronation Services* (1911).

—— 'Coronation Claims', in *The Genealogical Magazine*, vii. 510 ff.

—— 'Constables under the Norman Kings', *ibid.* (NS), vol. 38 (1923), pp. 113–27.

SANDERS, I. J., *Feudal Military Service in England* (1956).

SELDEN, J., *Titles of Honour* (2nd ed., London, 1631).

SHIRLEY, W. W., *Royal Letters* (RS), 2 vols.: i, *1216–35*, ii, *1236–72* (1862).

SQUIBB, G. D., *The High Court of Chivalry* (London, 1959).

Statutes of the Realm, 11 vols. (Rec. Comm., 1810–28).

STITT, F. B., 'A Dunstable Tournament, 1308–9', in *The Antiquaries Journal*, xxxii (1952), 202–3.

STUBBS, W., *The Constitutional History of England.*

TASWELL-LANGMEAD, *English Constitutional History,* ed. T. F. PLUCKNETT (1946).

THOMSON, W. S., *A Lincolnshire Assize Roll of 1298,* edited for the Lincolnshire Record Society as vol. 36 (1944).

THORPE, L., 'Maistre Richard: A Thirteenth Century Translator of the *De Re Militari* of Vegetius', in *Scriptorium,* vi (1950), 39–50.

TOUT, T. F., *The Political History of England (1216–1377)* (Longmans, 1901).

—— *Chapters in English Administrative History,* 6 vols., Manchester (1920–33).

—— *The Place of the Reign of Edward II in English History,* 2nd ed. (1936).

TREHARNE, R. F., 'The Baronial Reform Movement', in *T. R. Hist. Soc.* (1943).

—— 'The Knights in the Period of Rebellion and Reform', in *BIHR* (1948).

—— 'The Role of Simon de Montfort, 1258–65', being the Raleigh Lecture to the British Academy, 1954 (*Proc.* vol. x), 75–102.

TREVET, NICHOLAS, *Annales* to 1307, ed. T. Hog (English Historical Society, 1845).

TREVISA, *Polychronicon Ranulphi Higden,* with Trevisa's translation (RS 1865–86, 9 vols.), ed. C. Babington and J. R. Lumby.

TROKELOWE, *Chronicon: Johannis de Trokelowe et Henrici de Blaneforde Chronica et Annales, 1259–96* (RS, 1863–76).

VAUGHAN, R., *Matthew Paris* (Cambridge, 1958).

VINCENT, J. A. C., *Lancashire Lay Subsidies,* pub. by the Record Society for Lancashire and Cheshire, i (*1216–1307*), 1893.

WAGNER, Sir ANTHONY, *Catalogue of English Medieval Rolls of Arms* (Oxford, 1950).

—— *Heralds and Heraldry* (2nd ed., Oxford, 1956).

—— 'Sir Hilary Jenkinson on the Handwriting of Sir William Dugdale', in the *Journal of the Society of Archivists,* vol. ii, no. 4 (October 1961).

WALFORD, W. S., and PERCIVAL, C. S., 'Three Rolls of Arms of the Latter Part of the Thirteenth Century', in *Archaeologia,* vol. 39 (1864), i.e. (1) St. George's Roll *olim* Charles' Roll, 'E' in Papworth; (2) Society of Antiquaries 'Roll 17' *now* Charles' Roll, 'F' in Papworth; and (3) Walford's Roll.

WILLARD, J. F., and MORRIS, W. A., *The English Government at Work, 1327–1336* (Med. Acad. of America, 1940).

WILLS, DOROTHY, *The Estate Book of Henry de Bray* (Camden Society, 1916).

WRIGHT, C. E., 'Sir Edward Dering; a seventeenth century antiquary and his Saxon charters', in *The Early Culture of North West Europe*, ed. C. Fox and B. Dickins (Cambridge, 1950), pp. 369–93.

APPENDIX

(See p. 54 *supra*)

IN *The Book of Prests of the King's Wardrobe (1294–5)*, presented to Sir Goronwy Edwards (O.U.P. 1962), general editor E. B. Fryde, the following entries are found:

p. 27. MOREL REX. Nicholao Morel regi haraldorum percipienti per diem 7½*d.* pro vadiis suis per dictos 162 dies exceptis 15 diebus per quos vacavit per manus proprias apud Talebont 4*li.* 11*s.* 10½*d.* (and on p. 43).

p. 46. ROBERTUS PARVUS REX. Memd. quod R.P. rex haraldorum vacat in rotulo mareschalcie per totum annum presentem 23.

p. 156. Johanni de Mohaut menestrallo de prestito super vadiis suis quando est in curia per manus proprias apud Biriton' 17 die Julii 13*s.* 4*d.*

p. 164. MOREL REX. Colino Morel regi de prestito super vadiis per manus eiusdem domini ℞ ibidem eodem anno 13*s.* 4*d.* (and p. 169 20*s.* on 14 May at Talebont; p. 177 13*s.* 4*d.* on 6 October at Canterbury; and p. 181 13*s.* 4*d.* on 23 November at Winchelsea).

p. 185. Magistro Roberto Parvo regi haraldorum de prestito pro denariis quos debuit in fine vadiorum suorum de anno 22 pro prestitis factis eidem eodem anno ultra vadia sua quia habuit de prestito eodem anno 22 (et anno presenti 23) in tribus particulis 113(*s.* 4*d.*) et vadia sua non fuerunt nisi 4*li.* 13*s.* 1½*d.* et sic in fine compoti predicti idem debuit sicut predicitur 20*s.* 2½*d.*

INDEX

Abrincis, de, *see* Avranches.
Acre, siege of, 64.
— Edward I at, *see* Edward I.
Acton, John of, M.P., 152, 154.
ad vadia service, distinguished from service of contract, 104.
Alard family, 37.
— Gervase, 37.
— Justin, 37.
Alfonso IX of Castile, 25–26.
Alfonso (Sire Aunfons), eldest son (d. 1284) of Edward I, 62, 63.
aliens in England, 47 n. 5.
Alington (co. Kent), 77.
Almaine, Henry of, son of Richard of Cornwall, 44, 70.
— murdered at Viterbo (1270), 47, 49.
Alnwick (co. Northumb.), 16.
Amiens, Treaty of (1279), 48, 63.
Angus, Earl of, 92 n. 3.
Anjou, Geoffrey of, takes a bath (1180), 28.
Annesleye, John de, 154.
Antiquaries' Roll, Society of, 90 n. 1.
Apeldrefeld, Henry de, 154.
Appleby Castle (co. Westm.), 101.
Apocalypse, the Douce, 24.
Argentine, Sir Giles de, 33, 138.
—, Sir John de, 138.
Argentine, Richard de (d. 1314), 'King of the Greensward', 10.
armati, 22.
Armenia, the king of, 48.
—, envoys from, 63 n. 1.
armigeri, 22.
Arms, Assize of (1180), 109.
Arms, painted shields of, at Westminster, Winchester, and the Tower, 4.
—, in glass windows, at Rochester and Havering atte Bower, 4.
—, earliest examples of, 5.
—, tampered with, 9.

Arms, handwriting of, 11–12.
—, Rolls of, not used in detail: Boroughbridge (1322), 2; Cooke's *Ordinary* (*c.* 1340), 2, 24.
—, —, arrangement of, 3, 8.
—, —, not always in Roll form, 5 n. 2.
—, —, the PRA, 6, 7, 8, 11.
—, —, perhaps made in castles, 11.
—, —, interpolated, 6, 12.
—, — (incidental mentions):
Heralds' Roll, 7.
Collins' Roll, 8, 14 n. 1, 16.
Dering (*c.* 1278 ?), 11, 12, 13, 14.
Charles', 11.
PRA, 2, 5 n., 6, 7, 8, 11, 12, 13, 14.
Caerlaverock (1300), 13, 16.
Nativity Roll, 16.
Falkirk, 16.
—, Occasional Rolls of, *see* Caerlaverock, Dunstable, Falkirk, Galloway, Nativity Roll, Stirling.
Army: Terminology, 21–22. *See also* *armigeri*, *armati*, bachelors, bannerets, *dominus*, *equus coopertus*, esquires, *homines ad arma*, *miles simplex*, *servientes ad arma*, *scutiferi*, *strenuus*, troopers, *valletti*, yeomen.
Arras, Constable of, 82.
Arsic, Manasser (1166), 66.
—, —, custody of at Dover Castle, 84.
—, Robert (1212), 84.
Arthur, King, opening of his tomb (1278), 48.
Arthurian cult, 46, 49, 52–53.
Arundel, Earl of, contract for Falkirk, 104.
—, at Falkirk, 107.
—, at Dunstable tournament, 119.
Assasssins, the, 52.
Atholl, Earl of, 92 n. 3.
—, taken prisoner, 101,

maintenance, 125.
Malesmains, Thomas, 20.
Mamecestre, Simon de, 146.
Mameins, Nicholas of, 88.
Maminot custody, 66.
Maminot, Walkeling, 85.
—, Walchelin his son, 85.
Manchester, 23.
Mansel, John, 33.
Mapledurham Gurney (co. Berks.), 110.
March herald, 93.
Marchis, le Roy, 55, 57.
Marco Polo, 51 n. 6.
Mare anglicanum, 36.
Margaret, daughter of Eleanor of Castile, 57.
Margoth, the female spy, 58.
Marino, Mr., papal vice-chancellor, 28.
Marmion, John, 96 n. 1.
—, Philip, 96 n. 1.
—, William, 146.
Marshal inheritance in S. Wales, England, and Ireland, 90.
Marshal, Gilbert, Earl of Pembroke (d. 1241), 73.
—, Richard, 109.
—, William (d. 1219), Earl of Pembroke, 27.
Marshal, the Earl, (1234), 22, 32, 121.
—, — (Roger Bigod, b. 1235, surrd. 1302, d. 1306), 38, 106, 121–3.
Marshal, the Earl, and his deputies, 122.
—, —, the Fleet his prison, 122.
—, —, his harbingers, 123.
—, —, as purveyor, 134.
Marshalsea Court, 122.
Marshalship, the, 116 and n. 6.
—, in fee, 133.
Maunsel, Thomas, 80 n. 3.
Mauveysin, Henry, 151.
Menestralli, 54 ff. *See also* minstrels.
Menteith, Earl of, taken prisoner, 101.
Meules, *see* de Molis.
Middelton, Henry de, 123.
miles gregarius, 121.
miles simplex (bachelor), 23, 24, 26. *See also* bachelors.

Minstrel, the, at Acre, 52.
minstrels, German (1302–6), at English court, 60. *See also* Mohaut, John de.
Mohaut, John de, minstrel, at court, 166.
Molis (Meules), Nicholas de, 2 n. 1, 42 n. 2, 78.
—, —, constable of Dover (1258), 83.
Monmouth, 110.
Montague, Simon de, and his arms, 37.
—, Sir William de, 110.
Montfichet, Richard de, 119.
Montfort family, 78.
—, Amaury de, 90.
—, Eleanor de, 48.
—, —, marries Llewelyn (1278), 63.
—, Ralph de, 90.
—, —, Gwladys Ddu, his wife, 90.
—, Simon de, Earl of Leicester (1230, d. 1265), his career and position as Steward, 24 n. 2, 27, 42–45, 69.
—, —, his fellow crusaders, 42.
—, —, his sons, Henry and Simon, knighted by the Lord Edward, 25, 44.
—, —, his arms, 44.
—, —, Nicholas, his *barbitonsor*, 15, 55, 58.
—, —, Margoth, his female spy, 58.
—, —, his use of infantry, 109.
—, —, his *custodes*, 114.
Monthermer, Ralph de, 106, *and see* Gloucester.
Montibus, Ebulo de, 42 n. 2.
Morel, Nicholas (*al.* Colin Morel), herald king, 56, 57.
—, on holiday at Talybont (1294–5), 166.
Morris, Dr. J. E., on bannerets, 23.
—, —, in slight error on battle of Falkirk, 104.
—, —, on numbers at Falkirk, 107.
—, Dr. W. A., on sheriffs, 69 n. 4, 148 n. 4.
Morteyn, Robert, 42 n. 5, 96 n. 1.
—, William, 96 n. 1.
Mortimer, Edmund (d. 1381), 92 n. 1, 93.

St. Amand, Amaury de, 42 n. 3.
St. George's Roll (*olim* Charles' Roll, or 'E' in Papworth), 90–95.
St. John, John de, 66, 88.
—, le père, 115. *See also* Port.
St. Leonard's Hospital, York, 128 n. 6.
St. Omer, Thomas de, 157.
St. Pol, Count of, 82.
Salimbene, cited, 51.
Sandford, Nicholas de (d. 1252), 42.
Sandwich, Nicholas of, 84.
—, John of, 88.
—, Ralph of, 66, 85, 87.
—, sea-fight off (1217), 74, 82.
Saunzaver, Ralph, 151.
Savoy, Peter of (1256), 25, 43 n. 2, 72–74.
Say, Geoffrey de (d. 1216), 85.
—, William de (q.v.), 65, 66, 85.
—, —, his house in Dover Castle, 85, 87.
—, Geoffrey de (d. 1272/3), 85.
Scarborough Castle, 70.
Scirlee (Sch-), Ralph de, 157.
Scone, the Stone of, 100.
Scotland, King of (Alexander III, 1249–86), 25, 48.
Scottish border rolls, character of, 96.
Scures, John de, 146.
scutiferi, 21. See also *valletti*.
Segar's Roll (*c.* 1282), 63 n. 2.
Segrave family and arms, 142–4.
—, Henry, 33.
—, John, 143.
—, —, contract with the Earl Marshal (1297), 143 n. 3.
—, Nicholas, 123.
—, —, acting Marshal (March–August 1308), 133, 134, 141.
—, —, attests deed of Thomas of Lancaster (1319), 141.
—, —, quarrel with John de Cromwell (1305), 142.
—, —, imprisonment at Dover, 142–3.
—, —, pardoned, 143.
—, —, as a Lancastrian retainer, 143–4.
Selling, the Dean of, 127 n. 1.
Senescallus Anglie, 43–45.

Senescallus Anglie, arms of, 44.
Seneschal, William le, 157.
servientes ad arma, 22.
Seyton, John de, 157.
—, Mr. Roger de, 154.
sheriffs, social standing of, 148 n. 4, 152–3.
Shillingheld, Ivon of, 88 (? for Shillingford).
Ship Money, 35.
ships, the king's, 35–40.
Shropshire scutage roll, 65.
Sinclair, William, 101.
Siward, Richard, 2 n. 1, 101.
Skipton Castle, 124.
—, honour of, 128 n. 6.
Skyrewhit, Adam, 56.
Snowdonia, 110.
Somery, John de, 146.
Springhos, Roger, 157.
strenuus, 22.
Stafford, Sir Edmund de, his contract of 1297, 143.
Stamford, Statute of (1309), 72 n. 2, 136, 159.
—, Parliament at (1309), 136 n. 2.
—, a recognized tournament-field, 140.
Statute of Winchester, 18.
Statutum Armorum (1265), 5, 49, 124.
Statutum de Militibus (1278), 18.
Stewardship of England, *see Senescallus Anglie*.
Stewart, John, of Bonkill, 107 n. 1.
Stirling Bridge, English defeat at (10 Sept. 1297), 27, 106.
—, —, Roll of Arms of, 107.
—, campaign (1304), 113 n. 5.
— Castle, garrison of, 123.
—, siege of (30 May 1304), 13.
Stitt, Mr. F. B., on Dunstable tournament, 138–40.
Storton, Walter de, harper, 57.
Sussex, sheriffs of, 14, 64.
Styrcheslegh, Walter de, 154.
Swan Knight, *see* Tony.
Swans, Feast of the (1306), 13, 26 and n. 4, 28 and n. 1, 48, 49 and n. 2, 117, 118.

PRINTED IN GREAT BRITAIN
AT THE UNIVERSITY PRESS, OXFORD
BY VIVIAN RIDLER
PRINTER TO THE UNIVERSITY